RUNAWAY WORLD

MR. FRED MANGANO

Runaway World

MICHAEL GREEN

Principal, St John's College, Nottingham

INTER-VARSITY PRESS

INTER-VARSITY PRESS

Inter-Varsity Fellowship
39 Bedford Square, London WC1B 3EY

Inter-Varsity Press
Box F, Downers Grove, Illinois 60515

© INTER-VARSITY PRESS, LONDON
First Edition November 1968
Reprinted December 1968
Reprinted March 1969
Reprinted October 1969
Reprinted July 1970
Reprinted February 1972

UK ISBN O 85110 342 1

USA ISBN O 87784 688 x

US LIBRARY OF CONGRESS CATALOG CARD NO 74-78819

Biblical quotations are from the Revised Standard Version, copyrighted 1946
and 1952, *or from the New English Bible, New Testament* 1961, *unless
otherwise indicated.*

PRINTED AND BOUND IN ENGLAND BY
HAZELL WATSON AND VINEY LTD
AYLESBURY, BUCKS

CONTENTS

PREFACE

THE TITLE, though not the content, of this book was suggested to me by the Reith Lectures for 1967. Dr Edmund Leach, Provost of King's College, Cambridge, called them *A Runaway World?* in order to draw attention to the fact that the world seems to be getting out of the control of leading scientists and politicians. I have adapted the title in order to draw attention to an equally obvious feature in contemporary society—escapism. The ever-quickening rat race, the political double talk, the almost compulsive addiction to (and conditioning by) television, the endless preoccupation with sex, the glossing over the ugly fact of death are some of the ways in which our generation tries to 'get away from it all'. But the greatest unreality, the most comfortable mirage of our day, is commonly thought to be religion. Christianity, if it can hardly be accused any longer of being 'pie in the sky when you die' (for the churches, too, have grown dumb when it comes to talking realistically about death and what lies beyond it), is at any rate regarded as escapism by many people. 'It's all right for those that like that sort of thing', one hears it said; 'but I'm not the religious sort.' In other words, Christianity is the religious man's form of escaping from reality; it is his private way of 'getting away from it all'.

I believe this charge to be largely though not entirely false. Certainly we live in a runaway world, but for the most part it is not the Christians who are running away from reality. We have our escapists in the churches, no doubt. But this book is written in the conviction that the Christian faith itself is the very antithesis of escapism. It provides us with the most credible account of the universe and man's place in it, with the motive and the

7

dynamic for serving our fellow men, with the ability to face the harshest of situations with realism, and with a message of urgent relevance to the many who suspect Christians of escapism but are themselves running away from truth. The issue before us in this book resolves itself into this question: 'Who are the escapists?'

E. M. B. GREEN

CHAPTER ONE

RUNNING AWAY FROM HISTORY

Did Jesus ever live?

A MILITANTLY AGNOSTIC SIXTH-FORMER was some-what intrigued, and a little annoyed, by the fact that the captain of the school had recently become a decided and vocal Christian. So he accepted an invitation to go to an informal meeting in the house of a well-liked Christian master where the faith was to be discussed. He felt intellectually superior to the majority of others who were there, and was confident of his ability to show that the Jesus story was fictitious and the Gospel accounts highly unreliable.

It so happened that this young man left the house that evening in a very different frame of mind from that in which he entered it. But the position he originally held is not an uncommon one. Many young people today think that Christianity is 'a load of rubbish'. For example, the sickening sentimentality which surrounds the Christmas festivities each year confirms them in their conviction that in the nativity we have to do with a fairy story, something that does not belong to the real world. Those who really swallow this sort of thing must, they feel, prefer fantasy to fact.

It is not only schoolboys who regard Christianity as unhistorical. There has been a long line of rationalists who have argued that Jesus never lived, and that his cult is parallel to that of the equally mythical figures of Attis and Osiris. J. M. Robertson, for example, caused quite a stir at the beginning of the century when he argued the case for the Christ-myth in his books *Christianity and*

Mythology and *Pagan Christs*. Gilbert Murray favourably reviewed another such book by M. Couchoud, *The Enigma of Jesus*, and Bertrand Russell said he regarded the issue of whether Jesus ever lived as an open question. More recently John Allegro has gone on record as saying, 'The Church's misunderstanding of the origin of its cult began when it took the New Testament at its face value. Once you break it down into its Semitic sub-stratum you get close to the mystery, fertility cult, which is much more significant than we have ever given it credit for. There is no Jesus, or Joseph, or Mary left. You are dealing with myths. If there is any one personality involved, it is possibly some shadowy figure from the Essene sect, about a century earlier.'

This account was published by Vincent Mulchrone under banner headlines ('Drugs and the Christian prophets') in the *Daily Mail* in October 1967. He hails Mr Allegro as 'the calm empiricist who lectures in Old Testament and intertestamental studies at Manchester University' and gleefully calls him 'the most powerful scourge of Christianity since Pontius Pilate'. Now one does not expect unprejudiced writing from a newspaper columnist; how dull the papers would be if such a thing were possible! But an article of this sort does raise two points of interest. It shows that the idea of the Christ-myth is not dead. And it shows that some people are very anxious to believe that the Christian story is false, and are accordingly glad to make use of any shred of evidence which justifies their attitude. Unfortunately in this instance no evidence is given by Mr Allegro: we still await from his pen the 'astonishing discoveries' which will for ever discredit Christianity.

There is a further reason why this theory of the mythical nature of Christianity must be looked into seriously. As we shall see in chapter three, it has long been Communist policy to deny Jesus Christ's historical existence. An enormous number of people are subjected to this propaganda in Eastern Europe and Asia; it is very much a live issue. And it is interesting to notice how this became part of the Communist position. In 1842 a German theologian, Bruno Bauer, was deprived of his chair on account of his heterodox opinions. This greatly influenced Karl Marx, who not unnaturally thought he had been cruelly wronged by the bourgeois men of religion who dared not allow the shaky foundations of their house of faith to be investigated impartially. Now it was Bauer's view that the historical Jesus was a figment of the imagination of the evangelist Mark! It is one of the ironies of history (and a judgment on Liberal Protestantism) that the vagaries of a heterodox Christian and the sharp reaction of the orthodox should have laid the spiritual foundation for the most powerful atheistic régime the world has ever experienced.

Does history matter?

We are faced, then, with the question, *are* Christians running away from history? Before beginning to examine it, we must be clear that this is an absolutely crucial matter. Confucianism could survive even if it were proved beyond a shadow of doubt that Confucius never lived. It is his teaching that is important, not himself. The same is true, more or less, of all the great world religions apart from Judaism and Christianity: history is not important to them.

But with Christianity it is vital. For Christianity is not an ethical system which could be maintained regardless of whether Christ ever lived or not. No, it is basically good news about a unique historical person; someone who was born a mere generation before the evangelists wrote and was executed under the Roman procurator of Judaea, Pontius Pilate. He claimed to embody God's final self-disclosure to men. He backed up that claim by his matchless teaching, the moral miracle of his sinless life, and his well-substantiated resurrection from the grave.

Such, in brief, is the Christian story. There is nothing like it in the religions of the world. It has, indeed, features in common with the nature worship which underlay so many of the Eastern religions, based as this was on the annual cycle of the birth, maturity, death and resurrection of the year in its four seasons. The ancient Orient had many variations on this theme in the cults of Dionysus, Attis, Isis and Osiris, Cybele and Mithras; but with Christianity there was one fundamental difference. The Christian claim was attached, as none of these others was, to a recent historical figure, one known personally to some of the writers of the New Testament documents. This is what makes the Christian claim so stark and so challenging. It is all about the Jesus of history. Remove him from Christianity and nothing distinctive is left. Once disprove the historicity of Jesus Christ, and Christianity will collapse like a pack of cards. For it all depends on this fundamental conviction, that God was made manifest in human flesh. And that is a matter not of ideology or mythology but history. How well founded is this Christian claim?

PAGAN EVIDENCE ABOUT JESUS

One would not expect to find a great deal of early non-Christian evidence about the existence of an obscure peasant teacher in an unimportant frontier province of the Roman Empire. Roman historians and men of letters were normally upper-class people who thoroughly disapproved of Eastern religions; like Juvenal, they felt aggrieved that the Orontes had flowed into the Tiber, bringing a flood of decadent and very un-Roman superstitions in its wake. It would not be surprising if the humble birth of Christianity had gone entirely unnoticed by the historians of the period. But this is not the case.

Pliny

The fullest and most interesting account of Christianity from a pagan source comes from the pen of Pliny the Younger. He was sent by the Emperor Trajan to govern the province of Bithynia in Northern Turkey, in the year AD 112. We may be grateful for the fact that he had a typical bureaucratic mind, and wrote letters on every conceivable topic to the Emperor, no doubt lest he should be accused of possessing any personal initiative!

One of these letters concerns Christianity. He says that everywhere he went in his province, including villages and country districts, he found Christians. Moreover, their rapid spread had assumed the proportions of a major social problem. The pagan temples had had to close down for lack of customers; the sacred festivals had been discontinued, and all demand for sacrificial animals had ceased. Clearly Christianity was very much on the move by the end of the first century, even in so remote a province as this on the edge of the Roman world. Religious disapproval and economic opposition had not succeeded in checking its advance, until Pliny came on the scene and reported to his superior that it now seemed possible, under his capable supervision, to mend the situation! Those who persisted in their Christian faith he executed; such men were obviously contumacious, and deserved to die. But he confessed that he was perplexed about the nature of their crime. He had discovered from those who recanted in the face of his persecution that no enormities were practised in the Christian assemblies. Their whole guilt lay in this, that they refused to worship the imperial statue and the images of the gods, and were in the habit of meeting on a certain fixed day (*i.e.* Sunday) before it was light, when they sang in alternate verses a hymn to

Christ as God (*quasi deo*). They took an oath (? the baptismal promise) not to commit crime. Their lives were exemplary: you would not find fraud, adultery, theft or dishonesty among them. At their common meal they ate, not a murdered infant[1] but ordinary food. Pliny was perplexed by the apparent harmlessness of all this. Hence his letter to the Emperor.[2]

Tacitus

A contemporary of Pliny's was Cornelius Tacitus, the greatest historian of Imperial Rome. He tells us[3] how the Christians, hated by the populace for their 'crimes',[4] were made scapegoats for the Great Fire of AD 64 by the Emperor Nero. 'The name Christian', he writes, 'comes to them from Christ, who was executed in the reign of Tiberius by the Procurator Pontius Pilate; and the pernicious superstition, suppressed for a while, broke out afresh and spread not only through Judaea, the source of the malady, but even throughout Rome itself, where everything vile comes and is fêted.' It is clear that the patrician Tacitus has no sympathy for Christianity, practised as it was by the lower classes in general and orientals in particular. His evidence is, therefore, all the more valuable. He had good opportunity to get well informed about the origins of Christianity, for in AD 112 he was governor of Asia, where Christians were numerous. Indeed, he referred to them again in a lost book of his *Histories*, of which an excerpt has been preserved in a later writer. In it he recognizes the fact that the Christian

---

[1] The charge of cannibalism was often made against the Christians by the ignorant, no doubt because they spoke of 'feeding on Christ' in the Holy Communion.
[2] Pliny, *Epistles*, 10.96.
[3] *Annals*, 15.44.
[4] Christian emphasis on 'love' for brothers and sisters in Christ was given a sinister interpretation by the pagans; they suspected the church of incest as well as cannibalism.

faith originated as a sect within Judaism, though it was by his time quite distinct. And he gives the remarkable piece of information that the Roman general Titus hoped, by destroying the Temple at Jerusalem in AD 70, to put an end to both Christianity and Judaism, on the theory that if you cut the root, the plant will soon wither!

Writers of the stature of Pliny and Tacitus make the historicity of Jesus of Nazareth quite unambiguous. But can we go back any further? Is there any first-century witness to Jesus among the pagan writers? It so happens that there is a little.

Earlier testimony

To begin with, there is the statement by the Samaritan-born historian Thallus, who wrote in Rome about AD 52. His work is lost, but a fragment of it is preserved in the second-century writer Julius Africanus, who tells us, while discussing the darkness that fell when Jesus died on the cross (Mark 15:33), 'Thallus, in Book Three of his *History*, explains away the darkness as an eclipse of the sun – unreasonably as it seems to me.' Full marks to Julius Africanus for his objection; you cannot have a total eclipse of the sun when the moon is full, as it was at Passovertide when Jesus died. But the main interest of this quotation lies in showing that the circumstances surrounding the death of Jesus were well known in Rome as early as the middle of the first century, and were deemed worthy of comment by a non-Christian historian.

It is not only the cross of Jesus which was familiar to pagans in the capital in the fifties; so was the story of his resurrection, if we may judge by the probable significance of the following piece of evidence. A remarkable inscription has turned up, belonging to the time of Claudius Caesar, who was Emperor from AD 41 to 54.[5] In it he

---

[5] This is the latest the inscription can be dated. Some authorities assign it to the reign of Tiberius (AD 14–38).

expresses his displeasure at reports he has heard of the removal of the bodies of the dead from the tomb, and he gives warning that any further tampering with graves will incur nothing short of the death penalty. This inscription was found in Nazareth, of all places! Although it has been curiously neglected by theologians, Roman historians such as Professors Momigliano and Blaiklock regard this very sharp threat as the official reaction to the governor of Judaea's report on the crucifixion of Jesus and its sequel. It is difficult to imagine that Pilate could have avoided making a report to Rome; after all, Jesus had been executed as a political pretender, and such people were of very special interest to the Emperor. As a matter of fact, Tertullian, a Christian lawyer who lived in the second century, claimed that Pilate's report was still extant in the Imperial archives – though this is doubtful, for Tertullian was prone to exaggeration! Presumably any report Pilate made would have taken the line alluded to in Matthew 28:11ff., that the disciples of Jesus came and stole away the body while the soldiers who were supposed to be guarding the tomb slept. Hence, naturally enough, Claudius's sharp rejoinder.

Claudius was something of an antiquarian, and was particularly interested in matters of religion. A later papyrus has been discovered in which he takes the Jews of Alexandria to task for rioting with the Greeks, and is particularly incensed that 'certain other Jews' should have sailed down to North Africa from Syria and have 'fomented a universal plague' there among both the Jewish and Greek communities. This has been thought by many competent scholars to indicate the arrival of Christianity in Egypt (which must in any case have taken place around that time); if so, it was familiar to Claudius in the first year of his reign (it is hard to date the inscription any later). In other words, within a decade of the crucifixion, the Christian faith was known to the Emperor.

In any case, he was bound to take notice of it soon, for it created a problem much nearer home than Alexandria. Suetonius, a court official under Hadrian, and annalist of the Imperial House, records that Claudius expelled the Jews from Rome, because they were constantly making disturbances at the instigation of Chrestus.[6] The date, according to Orosius, was AD 49. Two of the people involved in this expulsion order were Aquila and Priscilla, who were Jews by birth but Christians by belief (Acts 18:2). It appears that Suetonius thought Chrestus (or Christus – the pronunciation was indistinguishable in Ancient as it is in Modern Greek) was the leader of one of the factions among the Jews; but clearly, the disturbances were caused by the preaching of Christ among the large Jewish community of the capital, particularly as his supporters would urge that he was still very much alive. We have in this slightly muddled report the echo of the tremendous impact made by Christian preaching among the 10,000 or so Jews of Rome, and the acute division in the ghetto caused by the proclamation of a Jesus who was no myth but a very recent and a very disturbing historical figure.

These men, Pliny (AD 61–114), Tacitus (AD 55–118?) and Suetonius (AD 69–140?) wrote of events which took place a mere thirty years before they were born; moreover their official position gave them access to good historical information. The evidence they give is more than sufficient to establish the historicity of Jesus, the author of this new religion, who suffered the supreme penalty under Pontius Pilate while the latter was administering the turbulent province of Judaea from AD 26 to 36.

[6] *Life of Claudius*, 25.4.

JEWISH EVIDENCE ABOUT JESUS

Here again the material is understandably sparse. We possess no contemporary Palestinian Jewish writings which might bear on the subject, and those which derive from after the Fall of Jerusalem in AD 70 are inevitably influenced by the split between the church and the synagogue which had by then become irrevocable. Furthermore, the Jews felt that the Christians were at least in part responsible for the affairs leading up to the disastrous Jewish war; they resented the fact that the church had not helped them in that life and death struggle against Rome; and they were not in the least pleased at the meteoric rise of the new faith, which gained a lot of ground initially as a movement within Judaism. For these and other reasons, relations between Judaism and Christianity were very poor by the end of the first century; and this fact prepares us for finding that there is not much about Christ in the Jewish writings, and that what there is is not complimentary.

Josephus

The most important witness is Josephus. He was one of the Jewish commanders in the war with Rome, and after AD 70 he set out to re-establish the credit of Judaism in the minds of Roman society in general and the Imperial family in particular. So he wrote his *Antiquities of the Jews* (published AD 93) and his *Jewish War* (published AD 75–79) in order to inform the Roman public more accurately about the religion of his fathers. These apologetic works naturally kept to the minimum any material that would irritate their Roman readers. Nevertheless we meet in the pages of Josephus many of the figures familiar from the New Testament: Pilate, Annas, Caiaphas, the Herods, Quirinius, Felix, Festus, and many others. Josephus tells us about John the Baptist as well, his preaching, baptizing and execution. James 'the brother of Jesus, the so-called Christ' has a good write-up.

But most significant of all is his extended reference to Jesus himself. 'And there arose about this time (*i.e.* Pilate's time, AD 26–36), Jesus, a wise man, if indeed we should call him a man; for he was a doer of marvellous deeds, a teacher of men who receive the truth with pleasure. He won over many Jews and also many Greeks. This man was the Messiah. And when Pilate had condemned him to the cross at the instigation of our own leaders, those who had loved him from the first did not cease. For he appeared to them on the third day alive again, as the holy prophets had predicted and said many other wonderful things about him. And even now the race of Christians, so named after him, has not yet died out.'[7]

This is of course a most surprising testimony to find in the pages of one who was not a Christian; but all attempts to impugn its authenticity can be said to have failed. It has as good attestation as anything in Josephus; it is included in all the manuscripts. We know that the fourth-century historian Eusebius read it in his copy of Josephus. He quoted it twice. No doubt some of it is sarcastic: 'if indeed we should call him a man' may allude to his divine claims, and 'this man was the Messiah' to the charge affixed to his cross, while the passage about the resurrection may merely be reflecting Christian propaganda. Be that as it may, we have in this passage of Josephus a powerful, independent testimony to the historical reality of Jesus of Nazareth. The stories about Jesus were no myth. They were so circumstantial and so well attested that they even found a place in this apologetic work of the Jewish Josephus; and he had the strongest possible reasons for keeping quiet about anything so inconvenient for his theme.

[7] *Antiquities*, 18.3.3.

The Mishnah

Other Jewish references can be found scattered sparsely around the Mishnah (the Jewish Law Code) and the Talmuds (Commentaries on these Laws). Jesus is called Jeshua ben Pantera which may either reflect the Jewish libel that Jesus was the product of an illegitimate union between Mary and a Roman soldier Panthera, or may be a corruption of the Greek word *parthenos* meaning 'virgin'. In either case it will refer to the birth of Jesus which was known to be unusual. The Jews knew all about the claim made for Jesus's birth from a virgin, and from the earliest days (when he was called 'the son of his mother' in Mark 6:3 – an unpardonable insult to a Jew), they put a sinister interpretation on it. But even this provides some sort of confirmation of the Christian claim that Jesus's birth was *different*. Similar corroboration is found in the saying of Rabbi Eliezer: 'Balaam looked forth and saw that there was a man, born of a woman, who should rise up and seek to make himself God, and cause the whole world to go astray . . . Give heed that you go not after that man; for it is written, God is not man that he should lie.. And if he says that he is God, he is a liar, and he will deceive and say that he is departing and will come again at the End. He says it, but he will not perform it.'

Such sentiments are characteristic of rabbinic opposition to Christianity. But consider what indirect attestation they afford to the Gospel story. Though Jesus is not referred to by name, it is obviously he who is referred to by 'born of a woman' and 'seek to make himself God'. The divine claims of Jesus and his assertion that he would come again at the end of the world are clearly reflected in this passage, as is the recognition that Jesus's purposes embrace the whole world and not Jewry alone.

There are other passages which could be mentioned; one makes a biting pun on the word gospel; another mentions Jesus's disciples; a third tells us that he performed miracles by means of magic which he learnt in Egypt. Jews never doubted the miracles of Jesus; but they attributed them to demonic agencies, as the Pharisees had done in the Gospels – 'by the prince of demons he casts out the demons' (Mark 3:22). Another passage records his execution: 'On the eve of Passover they hanged Jeshua of Nazareth.'

Enough has been said to show that there is some sort of Jewish support for the historicity, unusual birth, miracles, teaching, disciples, Messianic claims, crucifixion and reputed resurrection of Jesus, the author of the Christian faith. The Jewish evidence is well set out by a Jewish writer, Joseph Klausner, in *Jesus of Nazareth*, for those who want to examine the matter further.

The Dead Sea Scrolls

Before leaving this Jewish material, it is necessary to glance at the discoveries at Qumran and their bearing on Christianity, particularly in view of the wild claims put forward by two popular writers, Edmund Wilson and John Allegro, that the Dead Sea Scrolls have disproved Christianity.

The Scrolls come from a library hidden in the caves near the Dead Sea in AD. 68 when the community which produced them was wiped out by the invading Roman legions. There is evidence to show that this community had lived there for about a hundred years. From their own literature it is clear that they were a non-conformist baptizing sect of Judaism, zealous for purity, rather antagonistic to marriage, who lived apart in the wilderness monastery which has now been disclosed by excavations at Qumran.

Their fellowship was remarkable; they shared a com-

mon life, common meals, baths, money and quarters.
Each did his bit for the community. They were opposed
to the Temple authorities at Jerusalem whom they
regarded as renegades; they observed a different calen-
dar, and, like the prophets of old, they were convinced
that obedience to God mattered far more than sacrifice.
They lived in expectation of three Messianic figures, a
Prophet like Moses, an Anointed Priest and an Anointed
King.[8] These would wind up the present unsatisfactory
world order, and usher in the golden age, in which, of
course, the men of Qumran would have leading positions.
Pacifists until that great day, they would reserve themselves for the final battle between the sons of light and
the sons of darkness. Then they would fight.

It is practically certain that this community is to be
identified with the Essenes, of whom we have reports by
Philo and Josephus. They constituted the third great
party in first-century Judaism, along with the Pharisees
and Sadducees. Being a secret and monastic order little
enough had been known of them. But now, it would
seem, their main centre has been dug up, their library
discovered. Obviously this discovery has enormously
interesting implications for Christianity, for it sheds so
much light upon a little-known area of Judaism in the
time of Christ. But, as Professor Rowley put it, 'to suppose that the Scrolls can give us any evidence of the
nature of early Christianity is fantastic. They are pre-
Christian documents, which can only tell us about the
sect from which they came. They are highly relevant to
the background of Christianity . . . they enrich our
knowledge of the Jewish world at the time of Christ and
in the preceding two centuries. They give us a clearer
picture of a Jewish sect which was devout and lofty in

---

[8] These were, of course, three great strands of Old Testament
expectation. It is fascinating to reflect how all three were exemplified
in Jesus. What Qumran awaited, he was.

character, in which a true spirit of brotherhood prevailed. But they do not overthrow or confirm a single Christian doctrine. . . . They cannot be intelligently used for either Christian or anti-Christian propaganda. It would be as rational to study the biography of Pitt to find out the facts of the career of Lloyd George as to look to the literature of the Qumran sect to tell us about Jesus.'[9]

It is most regrettable to find a scholar of the technical ability of John Allegro running away from the evidence as he persists in doing. In 1956 he caused a furore by announcing on the BBC that previously unpublished texts from Qumran showed that the Teacher of Righteousness had been crucified by Alexander Jannaeus about 88 BC, and that his disciples expected his resurrection. At once five leading members of the international team engaged on deciphering the Scrolls wrote to *The Times* of 16 March dissociating themselves entirely from his views, asserting that they found no evidence in the texts to warrant Allegro's contentions, and concluding either that he had misread his sources or had deliberately made up a cock-and-bull story for which there was no evidence. Despite this rebuff Allegro continues from time to time to make tendentious statements of this sort. In an *Observer* Colour Supplement in 1965 he repeated his conjecture that what is recorded in the New Testament is a garbled version of what happened to the Teacher of Righteousness under Alexander Jannaeus, though there is not a shred of evidence that the Teacher of Righteousness was ever thought of in Messianic categories, let alone as divine; nor is there any suggestion in the documents that he was martyred, let alone crucified; or that his followers looked for his resurrection, let alone found it! Yet Allegro can say in that article, 'What little historical element there may be, then, in the New Testa-

[9] *The Dead Sea Scrolls and the New Testament*, pp. 30 f.

ment stories of Jesus, could possibly be a reminiscence of real Essene history.' Had he taken the trouble to consider the evidence afforded by Tacitus and Suetonius, Pliny and Josephus, to mention only non-Christian sources, he might not have got lost in a myth of his own making. In all charity one cannot help feeling that, on this occasion at least, it is not the Christian but the agnostic who is desperately looking for evidence to justify his prejudices. The charge of 'escapism' comes home to roost.

From this cursory survey of pagan and Jewish evidence relating to the rise of the Christian movement, it is clear that Jesus is no myth. There is no doubt that he really lived and died under Pontius Pilate. There is considerable, if garbled, support in these anti-Christian sources for the Christian evaluation of Jesus. This provides a useful check as we begin to examine the strictly Christian evidence.

ARCHAEOLOGICAL EVIDENCE ABOUT JESUS

Before we turn to the New Testament itself we might usefully consider some archaeological discoveries which shed light both on the beliefs of the earliest Christians about Jesus and on their testimony to Jesus. First, what can we learn of Christian beliefs from archaeology?

Finds which shed light on Christian belief
There is a fascinating acrostic, which appears in many places as a Christian symbol, notably twice among the ruins of Pompeii, a city destroyed by the eruption of Vesuvius in AD 79. Christians (mentioned in inscriptions there) were present in Pompeii before that. Acrostics were as popular in the ancient world as crosswords are today. This one was arranged in the shape of a square:

```
R O T A S
O P E R A
T E N E T
A R E P O
S A T O R
```

The straightforward meaning is unpromising: 'Arepo the sower holds the wheels with care(?).' But what is the hidden meaning which made it so congenial to the Christians? Here is the probable explanation.

In the first place, these letters add up to a repeated *Pater Noster* (the opening words of the Lord's prayer), with the addition of A and O twice:

```
            A
            P
            A
            T
            E
            R
A PATERNOSTER O
            O
            S
            T
            E
            R
            O
```

The implications of this are obvious. The address to God as Father stresses the unimaginable privilege felt by the early Christians in being adopted into his family through Jesus Christ. The cruciform shape emphasizes the centrality of the cross of Jesus, in itself as remarkable a thing as if a modern sect were to take as its badge a gallows.

The repeated A and O (or Alpha and Omega, the first and last letters of the Greek alphabet) expresses Christian belief in the cosmic significance of Jesus as both the origin and goal of the universe.

The second fact about this remarkable anagram that made it so acceptable to Christians seems to have been this. Where you have the A and the O you have a T in between them. Now the Greek T was the emblem of the cross in the early church[1]; for one thing, it looked like one. The placing of these T's suggests that they saw the cross of Christ as the mid-point of history, the central feature in the story of Jesus. Does that not anchor the 'Christ myth' very firmly in history, and sordid history at that?

The crossword enthusiast will probably have noticed that the word TENET ('he holds'), which, like the other four, is repeated in the square, makes the shape of a cross. Is this an accident? Does it not rather betray a remarkable conviction? 'He holds', he sustains. In the midst of terrible persecution, when Christians were set ablaze as living torches to light up Nero's gardens in AD 64, or when they were thrown alive to the lions in the Circus a little later, or facing the flow of lava that engulfed Pompeii – *he holds!* No mythology, that. Their assurance was based on sober history, the history of Jesus, the A and the O, who was executed in ghastly circumstances and yet rose triumphant. This was the ground for their confidence that the one who had conquered the grave could hold them, even in the jaws of death.

Another celebrated Christian symbol was the fish. It was used commonly in the early church as a mark of identification among Christians. It expresses very clearly and very succinctly what they believed about Jesus. The Greek word for fish is *ichthus*, and each of the five Greek letters stands for a word: *Iēsous Christos Theou Huios Sōtēr*;

[1] *The Epistle of Barnabas*, 9.8, makes great play with this symbolism.

'Jesus Christ, Son of God, Saviour.' *Jesus*, a historical person. *Christ*, the long awaited Jewish Messiah, to whom the prophets bore witness. *Son of God*, he was no mere man, but brought God into our world. *Saviour*, he rescues man from sin and death. That was a remarkably comprehensive creed, considering it had only five words in it! And notice how it bears out the point that Christianity is Christ. It is entirely taken up with him.

A third fascinating piece of very early evidence must have a mention. It has elicited considerable scholarly discussion, but has had little other publicity. The Israeli Professor Sukenik discovered in 1945 a sealed tomb outside Jerusalem, in a suburb called Talpioth. It had escaped spoliation, and its contents were intact. There were five ossuaries, or bone caskets, in the tomb, and the style of their decoration confirmed the indication of a coin found there that the tomb was closed in approximately AD 50. On two of these ossuaries the name of Jesus appears clearly; one reads, in Greek, *Iēsu Iou* ('Jesus, help'), the other, in Aramaic, *Yeshu' Aloth* (? 'Jesus, let him arise'). The theological implications of these crudely scratched inscriptions, written within twenty years of the crucifixion, are truly remarkable. They point to Jesus as the Lord of life, who can help even when a loved one has died. They point to Jesus as the risen Son of God, who can raise the Christian dead from their graves. It would be difficult to imagine any archaeological finds which could more clearly illustrate the burning faith of the early church in the Jesus whom many of them had known personally as a historical figure walking the streets of Palestine a few years previously.

Finds which shed light on New Testament testimony

Archaeology has also given us a great deal of light on the Gospels and Acts, again and again vindicating their reliability. Let us take a couple of examples from the

Gospel of John, which used to be regarded by critics as the latest and most unreliable of the Gospels. Chapter 5 tells of Jesus curing a paralysed man at the pool of Bethesda. The evangelist remarks that it had five porticos. No sign of this pool had ever been found in Jerusalem; moreover, no mention of it was to be found in any of the extant Hebrew literature. It seemed that John was spinning a good story that had no relation whatever to the facts.

But a few years ago the pool of Bethesda was discovered by a monk digging around the site of the Church of St Anne in Jerusalem. Excavation is still going on. But it is plainly a large and imposing structure, and it has five porticos. . . . What is more, mention of Bethesda has now been found in one of the Dead Sea Scrolls!

Again, in chapter 19, John tells us that Jesus was tried before Pilate at a place called The Pavement or, in Hebrew, *Gabbatha* (19:13). Nobody knew anything of any such pavement. It looked like embroidery on the simple tale of Christ's trial, until the French archaeologist Père Vincent triumphantly dug it up in the 1930s. It is the most moving memorial of first-century Jerusalem to be seen in the holy city today. It measured fifty yards square, and was the pavement of the Roman barracks. Buried under piles of rubble in the fall of Jerusalem in AD 70, it was not heard of again until its recent discovery. So John's tradition was seen to be no embroidery, but highly accurate information to which he could have had no access after AD 70.

There are many such instances where the accuracy of Luke has been vindicated. The writings of Sir William Ramsay, such as *Paul the Traveller and Roman Citizen* and *The Bearing of Recent Discovery on the Trustworthiness of the New Testament*, are particularly interesting on this subject. He began with the assumption that you could not believe a word Luke said unless it had independent testimony, but he was driven inexorably to the conclusion that Luke was the best historian since Thucydides. It is interesting to note how modern Roman historians prize Luke's Gospel and Acts as accurate, reliable historical material for understanding the first-century world. He is amazingly accurate, for example, over the complicated nomenclature of local officials; he never puts a foot wrong. He knows that Thessalonica has politarchs (Acts 17:6), Malta a 'first man' (28:7), Philippi two magistrates known as *stratēgoi* (16:20) and Ephesus an official called a *grammateus* or Recorder (19:35). All of these have been confirmed by inscriptions. The scenes he paints of Athens, Corinth, Ephesus and the journey to Rome ring absolutely true.

But perhaps the most amusing and significant turn up for the book is the case of Gallio. We are well informed about him, as it happens, for he was Seneca's brother, and the details of his career were so well documented by Seneca, Tacitus and others that there did not seem room for the proconsulship of Greece which Luke accorded him (Acts 18:12). There was much shaking of learned heads and mutterings about the unreliability of Luke, until an inscription was discovered which not only showed that Gallio was indeed proconsul, but even gave the year, AD 51. Thus what was once thought to be a mark of Luke's fertile imagination has become the lynchpin of New Testament chronology!

THE NEW TESTAMENT EVIDENCE ABOUT JESUS

The reliability of the manuscript tradition
As soon as we open the New Testament, a number of problems immediately present themselves.

In the first place, have we got the New Testament substantially as it was written, or has it been tampered with in succeeding centuries? It so happens that we are in a better position to answer this question with the New Testament than we are with any other ancient book. The gap between the writing of Thucydides' *History* and the oldest manuscript we possess of it is some 1,500 years. In the case of Tacitus it is 800 years. This does not worry classical scholars unduly. They do not doubt that the manuscript tradition is broadly reliable. Why, then, should anyone raise these doubts over the Christian documents? The answer lies, of course, in the magnitude of the issues involved; and fortunately the reliability of the New Testament manuscript tradition is exceptionally well attested.

In striking contrast to the paucity of manuscripts of the classics, we have thousands of biblical manuscripts, written in many languages and coming from all over the world. Although there are many variant readings in these manuscripts, there is not a single point of doctrine which hangs on a disputed reading, and the text is so sure that anybody who attempted to make conjectural emendations of it would be laughed out of court. Furthermore, our extant manuscripts are not separated by a great gap of hundreds of years from the autograph copies. We have the four Gospels in papyrus books written before AD 200, just over a century after the originals. We actually have a fragment of the Gospel of John which experts date as early as AD 125. A document called *The Unknown Gospel* was discovered a few years ago, written before AD 150, which draws heavily on our four Gospels, thus showing the authoritative position they had already attained by that time. The early heretic Valentinus, whose *Gospel of Truth*, written about AD 130, has even more recently come to light, quoted the New Testament writings extensively. So did the early Fathers Polycarp and Clement of Rome, thirty or forty years earlier. By the end of the first century, that is to say within the lifetime of some who had heard and known Jesus, the New

Testament was not only written, it was on the way to being collected. And from the outset it was regarded as authoritative information about Jesus. So authoritative that Christians quoted it with much the same reverence that they accorded to the Old Testament. So authoritative that the heretics knew they must quote it extensively if they were to have a hope of taking in any of the faithful with their particular heresy. This all enabled Professor Kenyon, the famous biblical archaeologist, to conclude, 'The interval between the dates of the original composition and the earliest extant evidence becomes so small as to be negligible, and the last foundation for any doubt that the Scriptures have come down to us substantially as they were written has now been removed.'[2]

The reliability of the Pauline teaching

But granted we have the New Testament as it left its authors, can we believe them? Does not Paul, for example, transform the simple human Jesus of the Gospels into a divine Saviour after the pattern of Hellenistic religion? This is a hoary old chestnut, which has often been answered, but it is worth considering briefly, partly because it has recently been revived in Hugh Schonfield's *Those Incredible Christians*, and, more important, because Paul's letters were written before the Gospels, and are, in fact, the earliest Christian writings we possess.

Paul was a Roman citizen, a Jewish rabbi of great piety and learning, and a violent opponent of Christianity. How he was converted to the faith he had tried to overthrow is a fascinating story in itself, and something, as Dr Johnson put it, 'to which infidelity has never been able to fabricate a specious answer'. But although he wrote independently of and prior to the four evangelists, his teaching accords remarkably with theirs. He knows

[2] *The Bible and Archaeology*, p. 288.

of the divine pre-existence of Jesus,[3] his real humanity,[4] his obedience to the Law,[5] his life of loving service,[6] his teaching,[7] his institution of the Holy Communion[8] and his death on the cross for man's forgiveness.[9] He can produce strong evidence for the resurrection, of which the Gospels make so much. He tells us in 1 Corinthians 15 of James, the unbelieving brother of Jesus who became a Christian because of the resurrection; of Peter who was convinced by it and transformed into an indefatigable missionary and martyr; of his own astonishing conversion to the risen Christ whom he encountered on the road to Damascus; and of the 'five hundred brethren at once' who saw Christ after his resurrection, and, though some had died by the time he wrote this letter in AD 53, most of them were still alive. They could, therefore, have refuted Paul if what he was teaching was not true. After all, they had known Jesus personally during his lifetime.

In this same chapter Paul refers to the very early Christian creed which he had passed on to the Corinthians. 'I delivered to you as of first importance what I also received,' he wrote, 'that Christ died for our sins in accordance with the scriptures, that he was buried, that he was raised on the third day in accordance with the scriptures.' Here we have a basic creed, which was *traditional* before Paul became a Christian only a few years after the crucifixion. Not much chance for myth to creep in here: and no conflict with the teaching of the earliest church. That is why Professor A. M. Hunter can write, after examining the subject with great care, 'The charge of Paul being the great innovator or corrupter of

---

[3] Col. 1:15; 2:9; Phil. 2:6; *cf.* Mk. 1:1; Mt. 1:23; 11:27; Jn. 1:1.
[4] Gal. 4:4; Rom. 1:4; *cf.* Lk. 2:52; Jn. 1:14; 4:6.
[5] Gal. 4:4; Mt. 5:17.
[6] 1 Cor. 13; Gal. 2:20; and *cf.* the whole of the Gospels.
[7] 1 Cor. 7:10; 9:14; *cf.* Mk. 10:10 f.; Lk. 10:7.
[8] 1 Cor. 11:23; *cf.* Mk. 14:22 ff.
[9] Rom. 3:24; 2 Cor. 5:19–21; *cf.* Mk. 10:45.

the gospel must be dropped for good and all. Original Paul certainly was, but the thing about which he wrote with such individuality and creative power was not his own discovery or his own invention. . . . He took it over from those who were in Christ before him. Is this not a conclusion of quite capital importance?'[1]

The reliability of the Gospels

What are we to make of the Gospels themselves? The great thing to remember is that they are an entirely new literary *genre*. Clearly, they are not biographies of Jesus. What biography would fail to tell us of any of the physical features or personal details of its hero, pass over 30 of his 33 (?) years without mention, and concentrate up to a half of its account on his death?

Equally obviously, they are not histories either, in the normally accepted sense of the word. The evangelists cheerfully bring God and his actions into the story, which would look odd in a history book. On the whole they are singularly lacking in interest in chronology or what is happening in the outside world.

The Gospels are basically a proclamation of good news; good news about Jesus whom the writers have come to believe is God's way of rescue for men.

This explains why the Christians did not write down their Gospels for some thirty years after the events they record. They were so busy preaching this gospel that they did not bother to put pen to paper. Writing was a laborious and expensive business before the day of the printing press, and was not valued in antiquity nearly as much as the spoken word. That is why for thirty years or so the Christian preaching was carried by word of mouth, until the eyewitnesses began to die off, and the Gospels were then written down to preserve the apostolic preaching for posterity.

[1] *Paul and his Predecessors*, p. 150.

But if they were written down so late, surely they are unreliable? Professor C. H. Dodd has shown in *The Apostolic Preaching and its Developments* that much the same pattern of preaching about Jesus can be found in all the different and independent strands which go to make up the New Testament. There can be little doubt that it faithfully represents the original Christian message. We can verify part of what the evangelists record. Professor H. E. W. Turner has drawn attention to some of the criteria for checking Gospel stories in his book *Historicity and the Gospels*. Thus, for instance, the survival of eye-witnesses to the time when the Gospels came into being guarantees, to some extent, the veracity of what they say. Again, the absence in the Gospels of the main concerns of the early church is a notable point in favour of their truthfulness. If the church had cooked up the contents of the Gospels we would have expected them to have put into Jesus's mouth matters of burning concern to themselves. But on the contrary, we find that these issues (the Lordship of Jesus, the Holy Spirit, the Jewish-Gentile split, the circumcision issue and so forth) are conspicuous by their absence.

Or, take the parables: it may be asked, can we be sure these go back to Jesus himself? Why should anyone pretend Jesus taught in parables if he did not? Who could have been the genius that made them up, anyway? Nobody that we know of in the early church taught in parables, but they knew Jesus had done so.

Or consider this test of the teaching of Jesus. The Aramaic experts have shown that a good deal of it can be retranslated into Aramaic, and when this has been done it falls into a poetic form which is highly memorable. This is why the retentive Eastern mind was able to remember it with such precision over the years and enshrine it in our Gospels. Scandinavian scholars like H. Riesenfeld and B. Gerhardsson have argued forcibly that Jesus formally instructed his disciples by heart, as the Jewish rabbis did, and that this teaching was conceived of as 'holy word' to be transmitted word-perfect to others. Hence, no doubt, many of the similarities in the Gospel accounts.

Faith and evidence

Some of the Gospel material, then, can indeed be checked in ways like these. But not all of it. Even if it could be, that would not make agnostics into believers. Kierkegaard in his book *Philosophical Fragments* expressed the point pungently when he observed that even if you had been able to keep as close to Jesus as the pilot fish keeps to the shark, so that you did not miss anything he did or said, that would not make you a disciple. Professor Bultmann made much the same point when he asserted, 'Nowhere in the New Testament can you get behind the Easter faith'. That is quite true. The writers of the New Testament were people who had believed in Jesus and who wrote to give the reasons for their belief. *Of course* their evidence does not compel belief. Evidence never does. Not long ago, when overwhelming evidence of the link between smoking and lung cancer was published in the press, there was one smoker I heard of who was so annoyed that he determined to give up reading the newspaper! Others have managed conveniently to forget it, and run away from this uncomfortable thought while continuing to smoke. But that is not the fault of the evidence. Evidence can never induce people to believe; it can only offer reasonable grounds for belief. That is the sort of evidence which the New Testament affords – reasonable grounds for belief. Nobody is forced to credit it: Pontius Pilate and the Pharisees did not believe, and they were not short of evidence. Similarly, there are plenty of able and intelligent men in our own day who do not believe. This, however, is not because the evidence is insufficient to warrant belief, but either because they have not examined it personally, or else because they are unwilling to commit themselves to Christian living on the strength of it.

An example of the intelligent atheist who apparently has not given much careful examination to the evidence of the New Testament is Bertrand Russell. To judge from his essay in *Why I am not a Christian* he can have given only the most cursory glance at what the New Testament actually says, or he would not be able to make such astonishingly naïve comments about Christianity. Nowhere, for instance, does he even begin to consider the evidence for the resurrection of Jesus Christ, which is the very cornerstone of the Christian position.

Aldous Huxley represents the other type of atheist who is unwilling, on his own admission, to commit himself to the demands of Christian living. He admits his own bias in a fascinating passage in *Ends and Means* (pp. 270 ff.) where he writes: 'I had motives for not wanting the world to have a meaning; consequently assumed that it had none, and was able without any difficulty to find satisfying reasons for this assumption. The philosopher who finds no meaning in the world is not concerned exclusively with a problem in pure metaphysics; he is also concerned to prove that there is no valid reason why he personally should not do as he wants to do, or why his friends should not seize political power and govern in the way that they find most advantageous to themselves. . . . For myself, the philosophy of meaninglessness was essentially an instrument of liberation, sexual and political.' It is not often that one gets as honest an admission of running away from the truth as that.

The evidence for the Christian case is very strong. Though incapable of compelling faith, it is quite sufficient to warrant it. And so it seemed to those first Christians, Jews to a man. Stark monotheists as they were, schooled in centuries of faith in the one God, they nevertheless felt themselves driven into this new faith by the facts which they wrote about in the New Testament. They slowly came to the conclusion that Jesus was not just a man, but God Almighty accommodating himself to human nature and living in their midst. The Gospels give us their testimony to what they found in Jesus Christ, and also the evidence on which they gave their allegiance to him.

A great many people who dismiss Christians as credulous escapists have never personally examined the grounds for the Christian claim. They have never read through the New Testament documents, and particularly the Gospels, with an open mind, willing to commit themselves to the One of whom that New Testament speaks if they are convinced intellectually by what they read. The young man with whose story I began this chapter was like that. But he had the honesty to realize that it was he and not the Christians who had been running away from the evidence. And after that evening he read through, carefully and critically, but openmindedly, one of the Gospels. It led him to faith. This was the effect wrought on E.V. Rieu by the enforced study of the Gospels which he did for the Penguin translation. This was the effect on J. B. Phillips when he came to study the Gospels at first hand and in depth, as he tells us in *Ring of Truth*. I remember a research scientist once saying to me that he thought the story of Jesus mythical. I asked him when he had last read it. He had to admit that it was a very long time ago. I said to him something like this. 'You are a scientist. You are accustomed to modifying your preconceived theories if the evidence warrants it. I suggest that you apply the same principle here. Examine the evidence at first hand. Be open to wherever it may lead you, and see what happens.'

I next met that man some months later in a Christian meeting. 'I did what you suggested,' he said; 'and it has made a Christian of me.'

His example is not a bad one to follow if you suspect that Christians are running away from the facts. At least it will show that you are not.

CHAPTER TWO

RUNNING AWAY FROM SCIENCE

The death of God

SIR RICHARD GREGORY, sometime Editor of *Nature*, was one of the unusual people who wrote his own epitaph. It ran like this:

> My grandfather preached the gospel of Christ,
> My father preached the gospel of Socialism,
> I preach the gospel of Science.

That attitude goes for an increasingly large proportion of mankind. The astonishing advances in technology, the breakthrough into the Atomic Era, the prospect of interplanetary travel have opened up unimagined vistas to the human spirit, and have induced such a feeling of self-confidence in the boundless abilities of man that the God hypothesis seems strangely dated and unreal. In this age of scientific humanism Christians are ridiculed for their old-fashioned, unscientific ideas. With their talk of God and Satan, of heaven and hell, of salvation and loss they are not only hopelessly off target, not only burbling complete irrelevancies, but simply deluding themselves. The man in the street reckons that science has killed religion: a good deal of what he sees on the television confirms him in that view, and a glance at the exterior of the church round the corner, its notice-board, its advertised activities and the people who go there, make it very clear to him that between scientific humanism and religion there is a yawning chasm: the one is modern and the other old-fashioned; the one works and the other manifestly does not. He knows where he is going to take his stand. And who can blame him?

Naturally, few men in the street are as coherent on the subject as this. They simply *assume* that the day of religion is over. The process has been going on for a long time. The free thinkers at the Congress of Liège in 1865 concluded, 'Science does not deny God, she makes him unnecessary.' Half a century earlier the astronomer Laplace had been rebuked by Napoleon for not bringing God into his theory of the heavenly bodies, and had replied 'Sire, I have no need of that hypothesis'. Today, as Martin Heidegger acutely observed, 'God's absence is not even noticed.' God is dead, and the scientists have presided at his obsequies. When Christians persist in their beliefs, they are simply running away from science. That is the charge.

Christian origins of science

Such an accusation would have sounded very strange to the scientific pioneers of the sixteenth and seventeenth centuries. For the truly remarkable thing about the growth of modern science is that it took place in a Christian civilization, recently liberated from the shackles of authoritarianism by the Renaissance and the Reformation. Moreover, it was pioneered by Christian men. Francis Bacon saw God's works in nature and his words in the Bible as the twin facets of his self-disclosure. So did Kepler, who revolutionized the astronomical prejudice of his day, derived from Plato, that there are only circular movements among the heavenly bodies. When he did his scientific study, he felt himself to be 'thinking God's thoughts after him'; he was, he felt, 'a high priest in the book of nature, religiously bound to alter not one jot or tittle of what it had pleased God to write down in it.' That is why he took very seriously the 8′ of divergence from the circular in Mars's orbit which he discovered by observation, and thereby paved the way for the reformation of astronomy.

Galileo and Copernicus remained devout Christian men, convinced that their work glorified God, despite the provocation afforded them by the obscurantism of the Catholic church of the day. Newton wrote his *Principia* in the assurance that 'this world could originate from nothing but the perfectly free will of God'. He is said to have spent more time in Bible study than in scientific research.

Robert Boyle, one of the founders of the Royal Society, was a sincere Christian, and endowed a lectureship for 'proving the Christian religion against notorious infidels'. Many of the other founders of the Royal Society shared Boyle's faith, men like Ward, Wallis, Wilkins and Barrow. They saw no contradiction in directing their studies equally 'to the glory of God' and 'to the advantage of the human race'. They would assuredly have seen nothing incongruous in the inscription over the gateway of the Cavendish Laboratory in Cambridge: 'The works of the Lord are great, sought out by all those who have pleasure therein.' Christianity was clearly not seen as escapism in those days.

But what of today? Is science still compatible with Christian faith?

Science, atheism and belief

It is a great mistake to suppose that scientists were believers in the sixteenth and seventeenth centuries, whereas they are an agnostic crowd nowadays. There have always been both atheists and Christians in the ranks of the sciences, as in other disciplines. There were many members of the Enlightenment in the eighteenth century who combined their empirical approach to reality with contempt for God. Men like Hume, Spencer and John Stuart Mill are among the architects of the atheistic humanism of our own day.

So when the Russian authorities decreed, after the Revolution, that the last relics of religious faith must be wiped out by scientific propaganda, on the assumption that religious notions will disappear of themselves once the true light of science dawns on men's minds, they were not doing anything new. Bishop Butler in the eighteenth century wryly complained in his *Analogy* that 'It is come, I know not how, to be taken for granted by many persons that Christianity is not so much as a subject of enquiry, but that it is now at length discovered to be fictitious. Accordingly they treated it as if in this present age this were an agreed point among all people of discernment, and nothing remained but to set it up as a principal subject of mirth and ridicule, as it were by way of reprisals for its having so long interrupted the pleasures of the world.'

It is an interesting reflection that within a few years of Butler writing those words in 1736, a religious revival began to sweep over England through the preaching of Wesley and Whitefield; the whole country was profoundly affected within a generation. There are not lacking signs that something of the sort may be on the way today. In Russia, China and East Germany Christianity, so far from dying at the advent of the technological revolution, is growing in outreach, depth and influence. Be that as it may, it is certainly the case that the sciences have always included, and still do, both decided Christians and avowed atheists. One has only to point to the contemporary Christian men whom I shall be quoting in the following pages, Professors Coulson, MacKay and Boyd, all of whom have written extensively both on their professional scientific subjects and on the relation of science to Christianity, to make the point without the possibility of cavil that a man may with complete honesty be in the top rank of scientists and also a dedicated Christian. This does not involve a dichotomy in the personality: it integrates the personality, as we shall see below.

Pride and prejudice

Granted that it is perfectly possible to be a good scientist and a good Christian, the question remains, why has there been so much opposition between Christianity and science over the past century or so? Why have relationships been bedevilled by so much misunderstanding and arrogance?

In its dealings with science the Christian church has often adopted a dogmatic attitude which has brought its cause into disrepute. Its opposition to Copernicus's heliocentric theory of the nature of the universe is a typical example. But the Christian believes – or should believe – that the God of grace is the God of nature, and that the truth in whatever area it emerges is to be welcomed as part of God's self-disclosure. That was certainly the attitude taken by the earliest scientists, and in it lies the only hope for our world.

The Bible is not a book of science. It is a book which speaks of the total relationship of man to man, to the universe, and to God. In so far as it enters into scientific fields, it does so in ordinary everyday language which speaks of the sun as 'rising' and the heavens as being 'up'. It is no part of the prerogative of the man of religion to prescribe to the scientist what he may believe about the physical universe on the grounds of a particular interpretation of the Bible. On the contrary, the Bible encourages us to believe that God meant man to be dominant over nature and to seek out the Creator's ways in his universe.

Accordingly, the Christian's proper attitude is to welcome the truth of God wherever it is displayed in his world. He will naturally expect it to cohere with the teaching of Scripture, because he is convinced that the one God of truth is the author of both; but if he finds real, rather than fancied discrepancies, he will do two things. He will, as a scientist, re-examine the implications he has drawn from his discovery; and he will, as a Christian, re-examine his own interpretation of Scripture.

Of course, the church has had no monopoly of arrogance and misunderstanding. The very success of the scientific method has so elated some of its practitioners that they have sometimes assumed that theirs was the only meaningful approach to reality, and anything that could not be measured or examined in a test tube was not real. Hence the widespread and boundless belief in the power of science to solve all our problems.

Bertrand Russell's approach is a good example of this sort of scientific arrogance. On the negative side, since science lends no support to the belief in God or immortality, these beliefs must be discarded, according to Russell, who prides himself on being the first to have introduced a really scientific philosophy. (He ought, with equal logic, to jettison *all* beliefs, values and intellectual reasonings. These things cannot be scientifically assessed – but this does not make them any the less real.) On the positive side, he has this to say of the power of science: 'Science can enable our grandchildren to live the good life, by giving them knowledge, self control, and characters productive of harmony rather than strife.'[1]

Such a statement looks peculiarly dated in the aftermath of two world wars and in the midst of the crime wave that has for a decade and more been sweeping Western Europe. Over-confident scientific optimism of that sort is quite unjustified and has not the least shred of evidence to support it. By their technological achievements men have indeed been able to tame the physical

[1] *Why I am not a Christian*, pp. 68 f.

44

world; but they have not begun to tame human nature. That is what makes the new powers we have discovered so terrifying.

The God of the gaps

If, then, mutual misunderstanding and arrogance on both sides constitute one of the factors that have gone far to wreck the relation of science to religion (for in reality these two are complementary and not contradictory approaches to the world), a second is the chronic tendency of Christians to claim room for God only in the areas where man's knowledge had not yet reached. This 'God of the gaps' is a pathetic travesty of the dynamic, infinite, all-pervasive God of the Bible, who is both immanent within every part of his universe ('in him all things hold together') and also immeasurably transcends our every conception ('dwelling in unapproachable light. No man has ever seen or ever can see him'). To shrink God until he is invoked only to cover the ever decreasing gaps in our knowledge is gravely misleading, indeed blasphemous. Such a God is too small.

One of the many strengths of Professor C. A. Coulson's splendid book *Science and Christian Belief* is the crushing blow he delivers to this sort of theology. It has had a long and disastrous history. As he points out, Newton himself was guilty of it, when he wrote, 'the diurnal rotations of the planets could not be derived from gravity, but require a divine arm to impress it on them.' This, as Professor Coulson points out, 'is asking for trouble. For as soon as any one possible scheme is devised whereby the planets might conceivably have obtained their angular momentum, the "divine arm" ceases to be needed; science has asserted its ownership over that much new territory.'

Either God is there in the whole universe and in every part of it, or he is not there at all. It was the mistake of the Rationalists to suppose that God's existence hung on whether he could be discerned in some part or other of the world – a fallacy perpetuated when the Russian astronaut Gagarin claimed that God is undoubtedly unreal because he was not to be seen during a journey round the world in space! It is a similar sort of mistake as to suppose that an artist is unreal unless room can be made for him somewhere in his canvas. The truth is rather that the canvas, though internally self-explanatory, would not be there at all but for the artist, who, more-over, gives some expression of himself in every detail of the picture.

The Bible has much to say about God's intimate relationship with the world. And it is not, as Professor MacKay has shown so clearly in *Science and Christian Faith Today*, the relationship of mechanic to machine; God is rather the One who holds the whole universe in being. He upholds the whole universe 'by his word of power', says Hebrews 1:3. 'In him we live and move and have our being' quotes Acts 17:28, 'since he himself gives to all men life and breath and everything' (Acts 17:25). 'Every single thing was created through, and for, him. He is both the first principle and the upholding principle of the whole scheme of creation' (Colossians 1:16, 17, Phillips). That and nothing less is the Christian conception of God. He is at work in the natural processes of growth just as he is present in human personality – for 'we are indeed his offspring' (Acts 17:29). And this creating and sustaining God, who is not less than personal (however much beyond personality he may be), desires a personal relationship with every man, woman and child in this world, as the beings who most nearly reflect his own nature, and yet have the power of rejecting him.

Three ways of knowing

It should be clear, then, that there need be no conflict

between scientific knowledge of the world and personal knowledge of God. Professor Boyd has pointed out with great clarity in *Can God be Known?* that we speak of 'knowledge' in at least three senses, mathematical, scientific and personal. He shows how each type of knowledge is similar in that it proceeds from presuppositions which are eminently sensible but cannot be demonstrated. Mathematical knowledge requires the assumption of axioms and of meaningfulness. Scientific knowledge requires the assumption of the existence of the external world and the uniformity of nature. Personal knowledge requires the assumption of other minds and personalities like our own. We are so accustomed to making the acts of faith which these assumptions demand that we do not even notice we are doing it.

Now whereas mathematical knowledge has no necessary relationship to the outside world, the other two types have. Scientific knowledge gives us an I-It relationship with the external world, while personal knowledge depends on an I-You encounter with other people. Fundamentally, science is concerned with description, and religion with encounter: science is concerned with the material aspect of things, but religion belongs to the world of personal relationships with the emphasis on the aspect of mind. Like all personal knowledge it is not merely encounter. It is encounter which issues in response – for without that response to the other person, you can never know him. Professor Boyd rightly shows that Christianity belongs to this third type of knowledge, personal relationship with, and personal response to, the Mind behind the universe.

God or chance?

It is precisely at this point that the atheist will feel that the whole question is being begged. *Is* there a Mind behind the universe? This is the nub of the problem; this is what divides Christian scientists from their agnostic or atheistic colleagues. Is there or is there not a universal Mind analogous to the human mind? Is there a God?

The question becomes most acute when we examine human nature. In a recent gathering of distinguished scientists and a few theologians at Windsor Castle to consider Science and Human Potentiality it became very clear that the division did not run between the theologians and the scientists, but between those who saw man as the product of a personal Creator, and those who saw him as the product of an entirely random collocation of atoms, a giant fluke.

These are, in fact, ultimately the only two possibilities. Either the Impersonal, given a great deal of time and a great deal of luck, produced the personal; or both the impersonal and the personal in the world are alike the product of an infinite, personal Creator. We have a straight choice between the position of atheistic humanism or the theism of the Judaeo-Christian tradition: nowhere else do you find the conception of an infinite personal Creator. Eastern religions have been strong on the 'infinite' but weak on the 'personal', with the result that the ideal is seen in terms of suppressing the personal in man and having it absorbed in the infinite impersonal. Classical Western religions have been strong on the personal aspect of their deities, but they have never risen to the conception of an infinite God. The Jewish and Christian faiths see God as *personal*, and in that respect man, in contrast to the animals, shares God's nature; and also as *infinite*, and in that respect man, in common with the animal world, is distinguished sharply from God by being finite.

This, then, is the choice: between an infinite, personal Creator and blind chance. Both positions are held by intelligent people. Neither is conclusively demonstrable. How, then, are we to reach a decision? Would we not be wise to consider the issue in a wider context, the areas of human value, human behaviour and human destiny, and see how the two notions fare then?

HUMAN VALUE

Christian and atheistic records

As the very name implies, most scientific humanists are extremely enthusiastic about man. Rightly so: *homo sum, nihil humani a me alienum puto* (I am a man: no human concern is irrelevant to me). Consequently humanists are keen on social and educational reform, on projects for the relief of need and the support of the aged, the hungry, the underprivileged and those suffering from war or racial discrimination. Recently, humanists have been in the van in matters of penal reform such as the death penalty, homosexuality and abortion. It must be freely admitted that sometimes the church has been on the side of the *status quo*, more sympathetic to the bosses than the workers, more concerned for social stability than humane policies. It is grievous to recall the wars waged in the past in the name of Christianity, the tortures of the Inquisition, and the gross injustices winked at by the church in the days of the Industrial Revolution.

Nevertheless, we must remember that not all men in power in professedly Christian States are Christian men, personally committed to the programme and the standards of Christ. Often the shameful things in church history have been perpetrated by bad men in high places in Christendom, not by genuine followers of Jesus Christ at all. It is, therefore, entirely unjust to say with Francis Williams in *The Humanist Frame* that Christian history is 'sodden with blood, torture and warfare'. There is another side to the story. It includes the social work of a Shaftesbury and a Barnardo, of a Booth and a Wilson Carlile. It includes the emancipation of women and slaves, the pioneer work in education and medicine, the foundation of the Trade Unions, and a world-wide concern for underprivileged people and underdeveloped countries which has no parallel in history. This concern has involved not only the preaching of the gospel of peace, integration and forgiveness to people who would otherwise have known only fear, superstition and immorality; but also the provision of education, medical care, and agricultural training all over the emerging countries of the world.

What the church has done to shape Africa in the nineteenth and twentieth centuries she did for Europe hundreds of years earlier. Where would our education be today without the Christian universities of Europe, founded in the Middle Ages? Where would our science be without the liberation of the mind and appreciation of God's world brought about by the Reformation? Would slavery ever have been abolished in Europe, let alone outside it, had it not been for the gospel of Jesus Christ which drove men like Wilberforce and Newton to battle against all the odds of conservatism and self-interest until this ugly blot on our society was removed?

It is only fair to ask atheistic humanists what they have to show of similar worth in terms of true, all-round, human well-being, to compare with this record of the church. Where are the humanists who are prepared to sacrifice their careers and comfort to go and live among the Dyaks of Borneo? Yet that is where you will find the Christians at work – still.

Humanists talk a great deal about the value of individuals: but they seem to love people better in the mass and at a distance than they do individually and when it costs. Such, at least, is the impression I have formed; I hope I am wrong, and will gladly own I am when I see a tenth of the dedication, sacrifice and selfless care for others, to be found in Christian voluntary societies the world over, displayed by atheist organizations for human welfare.

But even suppose that such an atheistic concern for the physical well-being of others, irrespective of age, race and usefulness for society, were incontrovertibly established, what of the other elements in human happiness? Do you go to Russia, China or East Germany today if you want to find free self-expression? Of course not. These are totalitarian régimes, and all opposition is ruthlessly quelled. Is that the highest way to show regard for human value – to shut men up in a cage? Christianity has always been implacably opposed to totalitarianism, because of its conviction that the State is accountable to God, and that men matter because they are made in the image of God. What comparable bastion can atheistic humanism offer against the stifling hand, the cruelty, the all-embracing demands of totalitarianism? If you don't believe me, think of recent events in Czechoslovakia.

The logic of the Christian value on man

If you ask why the Christian values man so highly, the answer is very simple. It is because we believe man is made in the image of a personal God, the Creator both of the universe and of its inhabitants. Thus man's freedom, his self-consciousness, his sense of values, his creativity, his heroism, his conscience, his love, all make sense; they derive from the personal God who is the source of our being. Similarly, our conceptions of truth, beauty, goodness and purpose derive from the God who enshrines them all. That is what makes man valuable; he is God's creation. That is why Christianity at its best has always cared passionately about all types and conditions of men. They matter to us, for they matter to God.

Christian philanthropy derives directly, of course, from the teaching and practice of Jesus himself. It was he who cared so much for the lepers that he did the unthinkable – and touched them. It was he who took pains to understand and cure the schizophrenic of Gadara whom everybody else thought beyond the pale. It was because of his example that Paul could say that in Christ 'there is neither Jew nor Greek, there is neither slave nor free, there is neither male nor female; for you are all one in Christ Jesus'. It was Jesus who both taught and exemplified this quality of love for all men, even his own murderers.

Nowhere does Jesus say a more emphatic 'yes' to every value put on man by the scientific humanist, than in the famous question: 'Are not sparrows two a penny? Yet without your Father's leave not one of them can fall to the ground. As for you, even the hairs of your head have all been counted. So have no fear; you are worth more than any number of sparrows.' But those words contain also a sharp 'no' to scientific humanism; it lies in the phrase 'without your Father's leave'. To Jesus the Fatherhood of God is the key to the whole question of personal value. People matter more than things because they are created and upheld by the Personal Source of all life. Here is a satisfying account of the world; it may not be demonstrable, but it is both intelligent and humane. It makes sense.

The illogicality of the atheistic value on man

But when we turn to enquire on what grounds the atheist values man so highly, the answer does not make good sense. Jesus had set a high value on persons *because* they were made by a personal God; the atheist professes high respect for persons *despite* the fact that they are the products of a quite impassive and impersonal universe. That is the irreconcilable difference between the Christian and the atheistic position.

It has always seemed to me utterly absurd for the atheist to profess such deep regard for the random products of a universe where chance is king. It is, I suppose, understandable enough to make this assumption in the Western world, which has been so moulded by Christian values; but it is none the less basically illogical. And it never surprises me to learn that atheistic humanism is utterly ruthless in torturing and eliminating unwanted people when it becomes the dominant philosophy in countries that have made a clean break with the Christian tradition, such as Hitler's Germany, Mao's China or Communist Russia. If man is the outcome of a fortuitous concourse of atoms, why on earth should you *not* manipulate him as you please, provided it is in your power to do so with impunity?

The credibility of the atheistic account of man

Let us look a little more closely at the credibility of the atheistic account of human nature and human origin. We are given to understand that life generated spontaneously as our earth cooled, and thus began the evolutionary process (subsequently advanced by chance and adaptation to environment) of which we are the end term – so far. To quote Bertrand Russell's famous 'hymn' to atheism in *A Free Man's Worship*: 'That man is the product of causes which had no prevision of the end they were achieving, that his origin, growth, hopes and fears, loves and beliefs are but the outcome of accidental collocation of atoms; that no fire, no heroism . . . can preserve an individual life beyond the grave . . . that the whole temple of man's achievement must inevitably be buried beneath the debris of a universe in ruins – all these things, if not quite beyond dispute, are yet so nearly certain that no philosophy which rejects them can hope to stand.'

In a recent paperback, *The Survival of God in the Scientific Age*, Dr Alan Isaacs wrote: 'the properties of the

ultimate particles which constitute the material universe
. . . spontaneously interact in certain ways and organize
themselves (without apparent outside intervention) into
units of increasing complexity. Eventually, after a
sufficient number of stages of organization, these attributes include those associated with life, thought and con-
sciousness. This process appears to be self-actuating,
self-perpetuating and reproducible. At no stage, therefore, is it necessary to postulate a divine intelligence.' In
other words, look upon the world as a closed mechanistic
system, and you will find no room for God in it. Precisely
what Democritus said in the fifth century BC! How could
you possibly find God in a closed system? How could
he possibly disclose himself? He is certainly not to be
boxed off in some small department. He is either the
author and sustainer of the whole thing, or he is non-
existent.

It seems to me that the position adopted by Dr Isaacs
and those like him, though impressive at first sight, is
none the less absurd, for the following three reasons.

In the first place, even granted the interaction between
particles, their spontaneous organization into more complex groups and so forth, we have still to answer the
prior question, 'How came they to be there at all? And
how is it that they come to be charged with such remarkable possibilities?' There is certainly no *scientific* evidence
in favour of such materialism. At the Conference on
Science and Human Potentiality to which I referred
above, none of the distinguished scientists present (mostly
Professors and Nobel Prizewinners) argued for it in my
hearing, though several, such as Sir Alistair Hardy, Sir
Lawrence Bragg, Professors Thorpe of Cambridge and
Hindmarsh of Newcastle postulated a Mind behind the
universe in addition to the matter of which it is composed.
Only so was it possible to account adequately for human
minds. I was reminded of Lord Kelvin's shrewd if over-

stated dictum, 'If you think strongly enough, you will be forced *by Science* to believe in God.'

Second, the type of view advanced by Russell and Isaacs gives no satisfactory explanation of aesthetics, ethics or freedom, as Socrates said long ago about the atomic theory of Democritus. It comes back to the problem of how you get ethics out of an unfeeling concourse of atoms, how you get personal being out of the impersonal, how you get freedom, or at any rate the illusion of freedom (if all is mechanistically determined), in a determinist world. Capable perhaps of giving an account of the physical world, materialist philosophy has failed completely to give a credible account of human nature. Man can make himself the object of his own reflection; he can communicate, love, think, pray. He is capable of the music of Beethoven, the painting of Rembrandt, the space-travel or heart transplantation of our own day. It requires considerable credulity to suppose that such a being arose by chance from a fortuitous concourse of atoms. The biologist Edward Conklin wrote not unfairly, 'The probability of life originating from accident is comparable to the probability of a dictionary resulting from an explosion in a printing works.'

My third difficulty about a view of this sort is a logical one. Even if it were true, there would be no reason to believe it to be true. In common with belief in God, this theory of the scientific humanist would be no more than the product of wandering atoms, as meaningless as everything else in a world devoid of meaning and purpose. Such a *reductio ad absurdum* is, surely, the desperate refuge of men determined to run away from the idea of God at any cost. It certainly cannot claim to be *rational*: indeed it destroys the very idea of rationality, while at the same time leading to utter agnosticism about the uniformity of nature and the power to observe it. Professor Paul Ramsey criticized this position acutely: 'If any viewpoint is ever known to be true, then nothing can be more certain than that man transcends nature in apprehending the truth about nature.' This transcending of nature is what gives men their value. Perhaps Jesus was being utterly realistic when he asserted that the value of a human being is in the last resort dependent upon his being made in the image of a loving Creator. It is, surely, this that gives men their dignity and worth. Once deny this, and the awful possibility opens up of reducing man to the level of a machine, of treating a person like a thing.

HUMAN BEHAVIOUR

Love, the greatest thing in the world

The good life is of common concern both to Christians and to scientific humanists. This is, in fact, an area where both can co-operate most helpfully together. Although there are some humanists who are unashamedly selfish, there are many who are not. Indeed, they often put to shame the lives of professing Christians by their social involvement, their caring for those in need, and their concern to banish superstition, advance knowledge and forward freedom. In all these respects they are following ideals which Jesus taught. Unfortunately Christians have not always been conspicuous in following these principles. There has indeed been much running away from truth, from social concern and from freedom in different areas and in different periods of the Christian church. This is something of which Christians have every reason to be ashamed. But it has not been the characteristic Christian attitude, and it was certainly not the attitude of Jesus. Whenever the church has not been notable for its love of people, its love for truth and its concern for social freedom and welfare, it has been untrue to the charter of its Founder.

New Testament Christianity has no time for the kill-joy attitude, the suspicion of food, drink, marriage and enjoyment generally which has sometimes masqueraded as the Christian attitude to life. Jesus taught that so far from making men's lives miserable, he had come to give them abundant life. In contrast to John the Baptist, he was no ascetic (Luke 7:33); he not only graced a marriage reception with his presence but supplied them with fresh wine (John 2:1–11). Paul dismisses opposition to marriage as a 'devil-inspired doctrine' and continues on this splendid positive note: 'God has made all these things to be received with gratitude by those who know the truth. For everything that God created is good, and nothing is to be rejected when it is taken with thanksgiving, since it is hallowed by God's own word and by prayer' (1 Timothy 4:3–5).

Again, love, the very corner-stone of humanist ethic, is equally the quintessence of the teaching of Jesus. 'Love your neighbour as yourself' is the necessary complement of 'Love the Lord your God with all your heart'. There is nothing romantic and escapist about such love. It is useless to say piously 'Lord, Lord' – unless the fruit of genuine goodness to others (particularly those unable to repay it) is seen in Christian lives: 'You will know them by their fruits.' What Jesus taught, he carried out in person. Never has anyone lived such a life of self-sacrifice and practical goodness to other people as did Jesus of Nazareth. And unless his followers share his love for people, his hatred of poverty and disease and ignorance no less than sin, then their religion is not the religion of Jesus, whatever they may claim.

But whereas the Christian enthusiastically endorses the humanist's emphasis on love as the norm of proper human behaviour, there are at least three questions he would want to raise: the basic questions Why? What? How?

Love: why bother?

First, then, why should a man love others, on the humanist view? It is by no means self-evident that a man should be unselfish, loving, kind and truthful. No doubt some muting of the aggressive and selfish instincts is necessary if men are to live together in any sort of community. But why anything more than that? Humanists such as Mrs Margaret Knight tell us that love is a self-evident moral axiom – but is this not the old naturalistic fallacy all over again? How do you derive what *ought to be* from what *is*? How do you get moral axioms out of a mechanistic universe? If there is no God, if there is no future life, if our characters are not, as Christians claim, the only things we take out of this life with us, then why bother? Why should a man not act like a perfect swine if he thinks that will make him happy? Humanists are agreed that happiness is the most desirable human goal. Why should a man renounce his personal selfish pleasures for the supposed good of others, for the happiness of those he has never seen and never will see – the starving in India or the dying in Vietnam? Upon what self-consistent principle can Sartre and Russell invoke *moral* arguments about war in Vietnam? If man is but the product of a fortuitous concourse of atoms, why should he get excited about the destruction of other such beings?

Fortunately, a great many who hold this view of the world are good and generous men. They are much better men than their theory warrants! They do care for the state of affairs in Vietnam and in India, because these are human tragedies and their own human compassion is aroused. Their very action pours the gravest suspicion upon their theory. Their theory has nothing to counteract the tremendous claims of self-interest in individuals and nations. But their loving actions speak louder than their rationalistic words. When men turn their back on God's revelation in Scripture he still sets the truth of it in their hearts. They cannot live consistently on their own premisses: they have too much humanity about them. And Christianity explains why. The truth is, surely, that man is indeed made in God's image. And much as he spoils it, man cannot utterly uproot that image from his being: he loves because love is one of the constituents of God's universe. It is, as the song has it, 'love that makes the world go round'.

Not only do Christians have a reasonable explanation for the universal recognition of the value of love; they have also an exceedingly powerful motive for reaching out in love to others, however costly it may prove. For Christianity asserts that lasting love to your neighbour is grounded in the recognition of God's love for you. 'We love, because he first loved us.' The sense of having been loved by God, although such love is utterly undeserved, is the mainspring of Christian love to others, however unlovely they may be. The Christian imperative 'love your neighbour as yourself' is firmly grounded in the Christian indicative, 'The Son of God . . . loved me and gave himself for me.' There is, therefore, nothing escapist or idealistic about Christian love. It is accounted for by the fact that, whether recognized or not, love is at the heart of the universe. And it is motivated by the fact that this love has loved us. Magnetized by this love, the Christian cannot but love others.

Love: what is it?

Second, I want to know what, on the humanist view, morality does in fact mean. In an impersonal and mechanistic world, all talk of love and morality is meaningless. There are no absolutes in such a world. All is relative. The good turns out to be what most people think to be desirable. The naturalistic fallacy which, as we saw above, derived what ought to be from what is, is increasingly evident in current sociological thinking and legislative proposals. What ought to be desired is discovered by examining what most people do in fact want. Morality is thus dissolved. No longer prescriptive (telling us what we ought to do), it has degenerated into the merely descriptive (telling us what the majority desire). This ethics by head-count is the death knell of all that we have known by morality. It is a category confusion of the utmost gravity. Yet what else is possible on the atheistic theory of the world? Whence are you to derive a moral imperative?

The more one reflects on it, the more terrifying a concept of morality this is seen to be. Though concern for people is professed, in reality the individual ceases to matter. Society is manipulated in the way the majority think fit, or the rulers decree (because that is what it comes to). But *quis custodiet ipsos custodes?* Who will keep an eye on Big Brother?

On the Christian view it is the individual who matters intensely to God; and society is improved by changed individuals, men who have been reconciled with God and are imbued with a new attitude of love and service to their neighbours. But for scientific humanism it is the collective which is important; the idea is that if you improve society — its education, standards of living, cultural pursuits, and so forth – you will improve the individuals within that society. Such a view is not only false, it is frightening. That was the doctrinaire attitude adopted by Nazi Germany, by Soviet Russia and by Communist China, with results we all know. The individual is sacrificed to the collective, and morality is jettisoned forthwith.

In point of fact, history shows us that morality does not long survive the decease of religion. Trotsky discovered this too late, when he was battered to death by those who pursued the amoral utilitarian principles he had himself inculcated. Lord Devlin spoke for many beside lawyers when he asserted, 'No society has been able to teach morality without religion.' Time and again throughout history the truth of this has been shown. Observe it in the history of both Greece and Rome: moral decline set in, despite the official advocacy of the highest ideals, when the fires of religion died. Observe it in the history of the Israelites: they abandoned God, and their morals at once decayed as they gave themselves over to the licence of nature worship. Observe it in the French Revolution, or in British history. In England moral depravity has consistently gone hand in hand with rejection of God. It was so at the Restoration; it was so in the eighteenth century; it is so today. Many thoughtful Germans recognize it to be true of their country: they trace a causal link between the rejection of God in the thirties and the horrors of Auschwitz in the forties. Emil Brunner put it like this: 'The feeling for the personal and the human which is the fruit of faith may outlive for a time the death of the roots from which it has grown. But this cannot last very long. As a rule the decay of religion works out in the second generation as moral rigidity and in the third generation as the breakdown of all morality. Humanity without religion has never been a historical force capable of resistance. Dehumanisation results.' Is that not true? Does it not emphasize that morality without absolutes, morality without God, is impossible in the long run?

Love: how is it possible?

Third, we must ask, how, on the humanist view, is morality to be achieved? Education and effort is no doubt the answer. But will this do the trick? Is it true that if you educate a man you will necessarily make him a better man? May you not make him a far more dangerous crook? What are we to conclude from the fact that the last two world wars took place between the most highly educated countries in the world? Plato's illusion, that once a man knows the truth he will inevitably follow it, has had an unhealthy crop of gullible adherents. It is simply not true. Plato himself came to realize this, after ruefully attempting to instil virtue by means of knowledge into the intractable young tyrant of Syracuse. Professor Joad made the same discovery, after a lifetime of passionate advocacy of the humanist position. In late middle age he recognized that education could not erase the tendency to evil in human nature – in his own nature — and he was honest enough to become a Christian on the strength of it. He says that those who, like himself, adhered to left-wing politics and rationalist philosophy had been mistaken in their shallow optimism about human nature, supposing 'that the millennium was just round the corner, waiting to be introduced by a society of adequately psycho-analysed, prosperous Socialists. It is because we rejected the doctrine of original sin that we on the Left were always being disappointed; disappointed by the refusal of people to be reasonable, by the subservience of intellect to emotion, by the failure of true Socialism to arrive, by the behaviour of nations and politicians, by the preference of the masses for Hollywood to Shakespeare, and for Mr Sinatra to Beethoven; above all, by the recurrent fact of war.' He tells us that he came to recognize that the evil in human nature could not be exorcized by a little more education or anything else. 'The more I knew of it, the more Christianity seemed to offer just that strength and assistance [I needed]. And with that, the rationalist-optimist philosophy, by the light of which I had hitherto done my best to live, came to seem intolerably trivial and superficial. . . . I abandoned it, and in abandoning it found myself a Christian.'[2] Those were

[2] *Recovery of Belief*, p. 82.

brave words by a man who had the courage to admit he had been running away from the truth for the best part of a lifetime.

If education will not deal with the evil in human nature, neither will effort: at least, not unaided effort. History is eloquent with the testimony of men who have tried to live the good life and have come to realize that it is beyond them. Herodotus admitted, 'It is one of the greatest woes among mortal men that although we attempt so much that is good, we do not achieve it.' Ovid put the matter pungently in his celebrated aphorism: 'I see the better course, and I approve it: but I follow the worse.' That is just the trouble. Indeed, it is worse than this. For all too often we do not even make the effort. A very able South African humanist undergraduate has been corresponding with me for some time. After hearing and being attracted by the Christian message she set her face against it and determined to face life on the atheistic hypothesis. She wrote to me: 'Why do I need God to control or help me control my faults? Shouldn't I rather strive to better myself? I've tried that for a year now, and succeeded mostly, except during exams. . . . I have tried to excuse this as abnormal but I can't. So I'll try harder.' Honest, and courageous, but it is not surprising that she wrote six months later, 'I feel so selfish always working and slaving only for myself, and even though I swore I could in the old days force myself to become a much nicer person, all through willpower, I find I can't. I'm too lazy, and I never get round to it.'

That is precisely what Rosalind Murray saw so clearly in her book *The Good Pagan's Failure*. The apostle Paul crystallized the problem in these memorable words: 'I do not do the good I want, but the evil I do not want is what I do.' The excellent advice of the moralist to love others is of course admirable, and may help some people. But the trouble is, we are self-centred by nature; we find that wrong comes more easily to us than right. What we need is not good advice but practical assistance. And that morality can never give.

But this is just where Christianity is so relevant. Jesus of Nazareth both taught the highest standards *and kept them*. The ideal man has lived. And Jesus told his followers that he would die for them, and in so doing take responsibility for their failures. Nor was that all. He would also rise from the grave, and come by his Spirit and take up residence within their very personalities, so as to work out in Christian lives (with their co-operation) something of the quality of his own life of love. This was the dynamic of the early church. 'Christ lives in me', they claimed; and their behaviour did not belie the claim. The God of love who has made this world not only expects love from us, but came in the person of Jesus Christ, to show us how this works out in a human life; and, as if that was not enough, he offers to enable men to reproduce something of Christ's own love in their lives if they will commit themselves to him. Is that not the answer to the perennial problem of human wickedness? Is it not the key to achieving that love which we all, humanist and Christian alike, know to be the only hope for the world?

HUMAN DESTINY

The humanist dilemma

When it comes to gazing into the crystal ball, and prophesying about the future of man, a radical split emerges among scientific humanists.

Some, like Professors Ayer and Huxley, are so carried away by the fabulous advances of science that they remain highly optimistic about the future. They recognize that all is not well with the human animal, but by improving the stock through the practice of eugenics and, perhaps, euthanasia, all may yet turn out for the best in the best of all possible worlds. Such men have confidence in the ultimate good sense of human beings; surely mankind will not do anything disastrous to the race, like engaging in cosmic war. Rather, they look to the day when the Welfare State will give way to the Fulfilment State, when mankind will have evolved into a global society, united, educated, prosperous and peaceful. Science, according to Alexander Comfort in *The Humanist Anthology*, is the key to making men good and bringing them to this desirable state 'by relatively simple adjustments in ways of living' – an astonishingly naïve hope! Presumably he refers to the efforts of the social scientists who may be expected to make great advances in the next half century. But, as Martin Buber exclaimed in disillusionment at the end of his life, 'Who can change that intractable thing, human nature? There is a tragedy at the heart of things.' This observation of his leads us to consider the second attitude towards the future to be found in the ranks of scientific humanists — pessimism.

This attitude is particularly common among those versed in the arts, the humanities and literature. Colin Wilson, for example, wrote a book, *The Outsider*, whose blurb tells us, correctly, that it is a profound enquiry into the sickness of mankind in the mid-twentieth century. And have you noticed how science fiction has changed its tune? No longer is it concerned optimistically with the possibility of human technical progress. That is now taken for granted. But it *is* concerned with the danger, the boredom, the sheer hell of the evolving human situation. Nobody writes Utopias any more. As literary men look into the future, they envisage something more along the lines of George Orwell's *1984*. The last of the long line of Utopia makers, which began with Plato in the fourth century BC, was H. G. Wells; but it is very interesting to note that at the end of his life he abandoned his expectations of a Utopia and threw up his hands in blank despair; for he saw the human race hell-bent on self-destruction. In his *Mind at the End of its Tether* Wells, who all his life had been preaching the perfectibility of human nature, at length gave way to the great wave of modern despair when he concluded, 'There is no way out, or round, or through.'

It goes without saying that Jean-Paul Sartre, Albert Camus, and the majority of the Existentialists, without doubt the most influential intellectual force in Europe today, have taken this attitude. Life is irrational, absurd, tragic; it is bound for chaos. That is their fundamental assumption. And there is plenty in the economic and political scene to justify it. But most of all, it is the enormous power for destruction, placed into human hands by scientific discovery, that makes so many thinking men very sceptical about man's chances of survival. When talking about the threatening 'cloud in the sky' for which atomic physics is responsible, Martin D'Arcy put the human predicament very clearly: 'The thought behind men's minds is that there is no future. In all past predicaments the worst conceivable was only a partial destruction or collapse, and human means could be thought of which could avert it. For the first time a monstrous weapon has been discovered which is not partial in its effects, nor can it be managed in the way past scientific discoveries could be turned to good.' He points out that a major war will not be between, say, the Russians and the Americans, but will be waged by powers like them against a common foe, humanity itself. He concludes, 'If this be so then we are facing a situation which has no alternatives; there is no longer any solution within history. The secular hope comes to an end, and neither the rationalist nor the positive historian has anything to say. Only the religious mind can find an alternative and a hope by relying on the God who is above history.'[3]

The Christian answer

What does the Christian religion have to say to this wide split among the humanists as they think about the future? Jesus Christ said both 'yes' and 'no' to each position.

To be sure, he shared the optimism of the hopeful humanists. He taught extensively about the 'kingdom of God', which certainly had a future consummation to it, in which lust, oppression and the beastliness of man to man would be done away, and all injustices righted; a kingdom where love would be the universal language and where harmonious relationships would exist among all the inhabitants. The corporate future of the children of God plays a most important part in the New Testament. But Jesus differed sharply from the humanists in asserting that unaided man cannot produce this Utopia. He put his finger unerringly on the basic fallacy of this way of thinking, which neglects the wickedness of man and regards evil as external and extrinsic – something that education, evolution and common sense will eradicate. With sterner realism Jesus pointed out that 'It is what comes out of a man that defiles him. For from inside, out of a man's heart, come evil thoughts, acts of fornication, of theft, murder, adultery, ruthless greed . . . slander, arrogance and folly; these evil things all come from inside, and they defile the man' (Mark 7:20 f.). Human wickedness is the intractable surd that wrecks the humanist's ideal for the future. Some of them recognize as much. Julian Huxley's blueprint for the future is qualified by the significant proviso, 'if only mankind as a whole could be educated to use it'. It was because they found that ideologies did not alter human nature

[3] *Communism and Christianity*, p. 165.

that Annie Besant abandoned the Rationalists after a lifetime in their cause, and Douglas Hyde left the ranks of the Communists after being on the editorial staff of the *Daily Worker*. Both were disillusioned on this very point, the intractable wickedness of human nature. Both came to assent to Jesus's estimate of human nature, and recognized that man is his own worst enemy.

But if Jesus Christ said both 'yes' and 'no' to the optimistic hopes of some humanists, he took precisely the same line towards the pessimistic estimate of human destiny adopted by others. He had no illusions about the destructive passions which lie caged, like wild animals, within a person. He knew that the logical outcome was ruin: indeed, he spoke more soberly and more frequently about the awful reality of hell than anyone else in the whole Bible. He had no misplaced faith in human nature. On the contrary we are told, 'Jesus did not trust himself to them, . . . for he himself knew what was in man' (John 2:24 f.). He unveiled the lust, squalor, greed and hypocrisy in the heart of Everyman as no teacher before or since has ever done.

Yet Jesus had to say an uncompromising 'no' to the pessimist. It is not true that ruin is inevitable, that there is 'no way out, or round, or through'. It is not true that human nature cannot be changed, that the power of evil habits cannot be snapped. Jesus did not merely assert these truths: he demonstrated them in the matchless life he lived in the face of grinding poverty, bitter and unprovoked opposition, deliberate misunderstanding, disloyalty, a mockery of a trial and a lingering, agonizing death. He endured the fiercest attacks of evil in his own person, and he overcame them, as on that cross he took responsibility for the guilt of a whole world at odds with its Maker.

The cross was not the end. The resurrection of Jesus Christ is as well attested as any event in history. I have examined some of the evidence in *Man Alive!* This resurrection is the ground for Christian confidence that in paying our debts he did not, so to speak, become bankrupt himself; that in facing the world's evil he was not engulfed by it. The solid ground of the resurrection of Jesus is the guarantee that Christianity is not escapism, and that Christians are not indulging in wish-fulfilment when they believe that God's will shall ultimately be done in this world as it is in heaven. The Christian hope for the future has none of the facile shutting of the eyes to the ugly side of human nature which humanists are often capable of; it is based on looking evil squarely in the face, seeing that one Man has overcome it, and believing that this Man is the head of a new race, whose destiny is to share his future. In Christ's resurrection we see foreshadowed the destiny of redeemed mankind. It is the one sure basis for Christian optimism.

This hope cannot, on any showing, be dismissed as mere individualistic wish-fulfilment. Who ever wanted an endless *quantity* of life until, with the coming of Jesus Christ, the possibility of a new *quality* of living appeared? He offered to give men here and now (as well as here-after) what he called 'eternal life'. Our experience of sharing this new dimension of life with Christ now is the pledge that it will not end at death. No, this hope is no mere wish-fulfilment. Nor is it selfish individualism. Jesus spoke of a whole world of men whom God made with infinite care, whom God redeemed at immeasurable cost when they had wilfully strayed from him, whom God loves so much that he is willing to share all eternity with them. His plan is for a great new society made up of sinful men and women who have accepted his royal pardon, who have been adopted into his royal family, and who have progressively been made more like his Son in character.

This account of man's destiny is no more demonstrable

than the picture painted by the scientific humanists. It cannot be proved, but it does make sense. It is utterly realistic, for it takes full account of the bad in man as well as the good. This, if you like, is Christian humanism; a view which sets a fantastic value on man as made by God to share life with God both here and hereafter, both personally and corporately. It gives a reasonable account of human morality, and, better still, it offers a new dynamic for keeping the standards which we recognize but, left to ourselves, so often fail to achieve. Finally, it gives a hope for human destiny which transcends disaster, a hope which is based on the solid assurance of the resurrection of Christ.

There is no escapism in such a creed. It is not the *Christian* humanists who have any cause to shut their eyes to uncomfortable facts either in the world around us or in human nature. But, convinced that both the world and mankind come from a loving Creator God, Christians believe that the supreme escapism is to attempt to live life on assumptions which leave him out.

CHAPTER THREE

RUNNING AWAY FROM REALITY

CHRISTIANITY IS OF ALL RELIGIONS the most earthy. It asserts that God actually immersed himself in human existence for thirty years or so in the first century of our era. It professes to make a profound difference to the way ordinary people behave in their daily lives. So to say that Christianity is escape from reality is a pretty damaging charge.

But that is precisely what people do say. Psychologists and Communists take the lead, and a great many ordinary people with no particular axe to grind agree with them: Christianity is an illusion. To be brutally frank, Christians are escapists, hiding their heads, ostrich-like, in the sands of religion, in order to remain cosily insulated from the stark realities of everyday life. Christianity is the religious man's world of fantasy, his particular type of escape hatch for getting away from it all.

Such is the charge. It merits most careful attention. The very fact that so many people believe this about the Christian faith suggests there may be some truth in it. I have no doubt that the church has its quota of escapists, like any other group of people. There are many weak characters who cannot face the reality of their position. There are plenty of Christians in psychiatric wards. There are also many nominal churchmen whose escapism takes a religious form: they call Jesus 'Lord, Lord' but have no intention of involving themselves in costly discipleship; Jesus called them 'wolves in sheep's clothing' of whom he would have to say on the Judgment Day, 'I never knew you.' But these various escapisms to be found among Christians do not, in themselves, invalidate Christianity. The vital question is this. Is there reason to suppose that Christianity itself is founded upon a fantasy world? Is the basis of the Christian faith so insubstantial that to believe it must be wishful thinking, sheer escapism? That is the question. It is a question which has been put with great force by two giants of the nineteenth century, Marx and Freud. It is a question which demands an answer.

RELIGION: THE OPIATE OF THE PEOPLE?

The Marxist charge

Communists, following Karl Marx, regard religion in general, and Christianity in particular, as a soporific drug administered by the bourgeoisie to keep the workers docile when they should be rising up in rebellion to shake off their chains. Karl Marx observed the appalling social injustices which went on unchecked in supposedly Christian England in the last century; he saw that the victims of injustice in this life were assured by the churches of bliss in the next, and in righteous resentment he coined the famous statement, 'Religion is the opiate of the people'. He saw it as the illusory compensation offered to the oppressed, the bogus palliative for the ills of a hopelessly perverted society; and he maintained that religion would die a natural death as soon as true socialism came in.

No-one could deny that Marx had plenty of justification for coming to this conclusion. There was sickening hypocrisy in Victorian religion, which often appears to have been a sop offered by the exploiters to the exploited. But the best preachers of the day were just as vehement as Marx himself in denouncing this state of affairs. They were well aware that Christianity has strong social implications. Charles Spurgeon had thousands flocking to his church each week; he was constant in his attack on formalism and hypocrisy in religion. He castigated employers who cheated their workers and snobs who indulged in class distinction. This should not in the least surprise us: after all, both are lambasted in the Epistle of James in the New Testament, not to mention the books of the Old Testament, where matters of social justice occupied the attention of the prophets more than any other single theme. In the last century the 'conformists' went to church; today they stay away. This means that there were large numbers of 'hangers on' in the Victorian churches who remained untouched by the spirit and attitudes of true Christianity.

But there is nothing more shattering in the teaching of Jesus than his biting invective against formalism, which was as rife then as it was in Victorian England. There certainly was a religion which was the opiate of the people in the first century, and Jesus was scathing in his denunciation of those who dispensed it. 'You devour widows' houses and for a pretence you make long prayers', he said. 'Woe to you, hypocrites, . . . how are you to escape being sentenced to hell?' He compared them to their cherished whitewashed tombs, beautiful enough on the outside but revolting within. Ought not Marx to have remembered that, so far from detracting from the value of the genuine article, the existence of counterfeits enhances it?

It was indeed a ghastly thing that little children had to climb up chimneys to clean them for a fifteen-hour day at derisory wages in a country that professed the Christian faith. But during the Industrial Revolution something verging on absolute power became vested in comparatively few men. And they demonstrated the truth of Lord Acton's dictum, 'All power tends to corrupt: absolute power tends to corrupt absolutely.' What the horrors perpetrated in the last century really show is not that religion is dope, but that no man is good enough to be allowed absolute power over anyone else. And that is a thesis which is Christian through and through: man has a sinister twist in his nature, and without the power of Christ to counteract this, he is likely to become increasingly self-centred. The ugly results of human self-centredness are equally evident in capitalist and in Communist societies. One has only to recall the atrocities of Russian leaders to appreciate both the falsity of the Communist theory that once you remove the economic injustices from society men will behave well, and the truth of the Christian claim that all men suffer from the disease of self-will to which Christ provides if not the total cure (in this life) at least the antidote.

The Marxist mistake

Karl Marx never examined Christianity with any care. He was wilfully blind, in fact, to the historical evidence. Not bothering to look into it for himself, he swallowed the absurd theories about Christian origins put forward by Strauss and Bauer which have many times been decisively refuted. The fantastic thing is that they still figure in Communist propaganda. Christianity arose in the second century AD as a revolt of the masses; Jesus was a mythological figure, and nobody tried to claim his historicity until the middle of the second century; the New Testament writings arose mostly in the second century too, and are totally unreliable. This is the sort of rubbish which is churned out with parrot-like regularity even in comparatively serious atheistic journals like *Sputnik Ateista*. It comes straight out of Karl Marx, and it is laughably untrue.

The view that Christianity was a mass movement arising from the frustrations of the common man in the war-weary world of the mid-second century is a particularly unfortunate gaffe on Marx's part: that age was one of the most prosperous, contented and stable periods in history! And so far from being a drug to dull the pain of agonized society, Christianity brought to the ancient world a most powerful injection of social equality. Here was a religion which preached that masters and slaves were on precisely the same footing before God. The former would have to give account to their Master in heaven of how they had treated their slaves; the latter were to work to please their heavenly Master, not just to get by with their earthly boss. What is more, the Christians acted on this belief. Master and slave were knit together in a bond of love for each other and for Christ who had forgiven them. This love eventually led to the breakdown of class distinction in the Empire. In the meantime, it produced an attitude like that of Paul in his letter to Philemon, the owner of the criminal runaway slave Onesimus. Paul had led this man to faith in Christ, just as he had earlier been instrumental in the conversion of Philemon; and he wrote to the latter asking him to receive Onesimus 'no longer as a slave, but . . . as a dear brother, very dear indeed to me and how much dearer to you, both as man and as Christian' (Philemon 16). Not much opiate about that sort of religion!

Unfortunately, Marx never knew what genuine religion was about. Reared in a family which changed its religion as a matter of convenience, brought up in a circle which amused itself by pulling the New Testament to pieces, he had to eke out a precarious living at a time when the state church was practically synonymous with the forces of reaction. No wonder he thought religion the opiate of the people. Christianity is not the drug he thought it was, but the accident of history by which Marx grew up in surroundings where the church was so far astray from its moorings has had world-wide repercussions. Christians must face this with humility and shame as they hold dialogue with Communists. Marx did get the wrong end of the stick about the Christian faith; but it was by no means all his fault.

Communist persecution

The Communists have enthusiastically taken up Marx's views on Christianity. Lenin thought it a deliberate attempt by the ruling classes to keep the masses subservient (in the hopes of a heavenly reward), whilst they themselves salved their consciences by engaging in a little philanthropy. This, he wrote, offered them 'cheap justification for all their exploiting' and 'low price tickets to heavenly bliss'. He originally reckoned that it was not necessary to repress religion; it would die naturally when the social conditions which gave rise to it had been revolutionized. But soon persecution set in; religion was poison running through the veins of society, and a crusade must be launched against it. In the fifty years of Communist rule Soviet governments have wavered between these two admittedly contradictory attitudes to Christianity. Surely one or other of these policies should have worked, if their assessment of religion is correct.

The Communist hatred of religion is, of course, very understandable. The Russian Orthodox Church was in a terrible state at the beginning of the twentieth century. It appeared to be a mere tool in the hands of the Czar, and was implicated in some of the most appalling abuses of government and oppression of the poor. Ghastly crimes were perpetrated under the aegis of the church. Here, surely, was ample justification for the Marxist–Leninist view of religion. Could such a guilty institution survive?

The revolutionaries were persuaded that it could not. Accordingly, early in 1918 all church property was confiscated, priests disenfranchized, seminaries closed, religious teaching except inside church buildings for-

bidden, Christian marriage replaced by a civil ceremony
– and the church was left to die. But the church refused
to die. Persecution was therefore added as early as 1921
in order to accelerate the process; in 1929 it was one of
the main aims of the first Five Year Plan, and so it has
continued, with a few intermissions, ever since. One of
these periods of relaxation was the Second World War.
During the rigours of the German invasion churches were
reopened, museums of atheism closed, church bells heard
again on the radio, and the whole country called to
prayer! Then with Stalin's savage repressive measures
after the war, the battle against this obstinate illusion of
Christianity was joined again. The story is well told in
Michael Bordeaux's book, *Opium of the People*, and Nikita
Struve's *Christians in Contemporary Russia*. These books
show the vicious methods in force against the Christians,
and the intense atheist propaganda which is disseminated
in Russia, while there is, of course, no right to reply. But
has the church collapsed? Far from it. It is stronger than
ever. The Baptists and the Orthodox (purged and refined
by all they have been through) are both flourishing –
like hardy oak trees in a winter storm. The Bolshevik
theory that religion was illusory, the prop of a decadent
capitalist society, has been proved wrong. As Dostoevsky
wrote in *The Idiot*, 'The religious instinct will not succumb
to any argument or to any form of atheism.'

One cannot help feeling that many Communists know
in their heart of hearts that they are running away from
the truth by this senseless persecution of religion. The
return of Stalin's own daughter, Svetlana, to religious
faith speaks volumes for what is going on in thoughtful
circles in the USSR. It reminds one of the resilience of
Christianity in Germany after the determined attempts
of the Nazis to suppress it. Ironically enough, Hitler's
headquarters in Berlin are now a Christian chapel.
Hitler's lieutenant, Martin Bormann, was passionately

anti-Christian. During the War he wrote home to his wife, 'See that none of our children get corrupted by that poison, Christianity.' Today seven of his nine children are decided Christians; at least one of them is a missionary.

Communist escapism

History is strewn with the graves of those who have thought to bury the church. It would seem that the Russian authorities sense this; for they are remarkably unwilling to face the evidence about Christianity. Bibles are strictly forbidden. Debates with believers are frowned on; they could lead to conversions, and frequently do.

Michael Bordeaux draws attention to the fact that 'no atheist ringleader has ever dared allow those under him to study the Bible, even for the purpose of spying out the enemy's territory in order to conquer it'. He records his own distress at the sheer intellectual dishonesty of Alexander Osipov, the Leningrad Professor of Old Testament who apostasized and became the régime's prize exhibit in the campaign against religion. In answer to Bordeaux's question asking how a biblical scholar like himself could completely ignore the historic person of Jesus in his lecture, Osipov replied that Jesus Christ had never lived: this had been virtually proved by the discovery of the Dead Sea Scrolls. The Christian story, he continued, was merely one version of the Near-Eastern myth about a dying and rising god and was invented by the early church to compensate for their privations at the hands of the Romans. This cock-and-bull story, as Bordeaux points out, would have been simply laughable if the Russian public had any access to the Scrolls: but, of course, they are not published in Russia.

The whole sad incident underlines the unwillingness of the Communists to examine evidence on this matter. They are running away from reality. Recently Moscow

Radio had to abandon an advertised broadcast attacking Christianity as a source of immorality (the official party line) because nobody could be found to sustain the argument! The escapist attitude that is disclosed by incidents such as this hardly adds weight to their theory that Christians are the people who are running away. And it distresses some honest atheists, as the following quotation shows: 'What impresses me . . . is that atheism today seems to have given up the search for truth. Facts and arguments which tell against it are dismissed in silence.'[1]

The Marxist attack on religion is itself a form of escapism. The very intensity of their persecution of Christians is some evidence of a bad conscience about this flight from reality into fantasy. Eugène Lyons, once an ardent Communist, has shown in his celebrated *Workers' Paradise Lost* the many respects in which Communism clings to illusions in the face of unpalatable facts. Once an ardent admirer of Communism, he has left their camp, bitterly disappointed. Many of Douglas Hyde's friends were forced into a similar position by sheer disillusionment. But he himself left Communism for Christianity; and he is in no doubt that he left the world of illusion for the world of reality. For many years News Editor of the *Daily Worker*, he wrote as follows in his book, *I Believed*: 'Six men who like me were Communists or fellow travellers, and who left the Movement disillusioned, called their story "The God that failed". They lost a faith, though it was a bad one, and in most cases found only a vacuum. I was more fortunate. I lost my Communism because I had been shown something better. I did not find it easy to get to know my new God . . . But one thing is certain. My God has not failed.'

---

[1] *Christians in Contemporary Russia* by Nikita Struve, p. 288.

RELIGION: THE FUTURE OF AN ILLUSION?

The future of an illusion

You do not have to dabble very deep in psychology before coming across Freud's view of religion as an obsessional neurosis. He wrote several books about it, the most trenchant being entitled *The Future of an Illusion*. He believed that when Christians talk about their heavenly Father, all they are doing is to project into the empty skies their image of their own father. This illusion arises from the subconscious need for protection and comfort once a person outgrows the childhood phase in his own home. Freud believed that in psychoanalysis he had found the answer to this universal neurosis.

His position, which is often thoughtlessly adopted by those who know little of psychology and less of the Christian faith, exposes itself to a number of criticisms. For one thing, Freud was as ignorant of genuine Christianity as was Karl Marx. He spent all his time among the abnormal and mentally ill, and this inevitably influenced his judgment.

This occupational hazard had an important consequence. He quite failed to distinguish between religious fantasy as observed in the mentally sick, and religion as an eminently reasonable attitude to life adopted by a very large number of healthy and intelligent people. Once you start accepting an abnormal person's view as the criterion of truth in religion, you might as well accept the reliability of his evaluation of everything else—including the usefulness of psychiatry! W. B. Selbie said very truly, if not very kindly, in his *Christianity and the New Psychology*, 'Many of the psychologists are living in a fantasy world of their own, and the kind of religion they are dealing with is largely the product of their own not very healthy imaginations.' One might add in passing that this criticism would apply to Jung as well as to

Freud. He assumed that Christianity was an amalgam of fantasy and emotionalism, and he was forced to justify this assumption by asserting that we know nothing of the Jesus of history – a brand of escapism which we examined in chapter one.

A further difficulty in the position which Freud maintained, and which has had such wide repercussions, is the boomerang nature of the argument. He writes off Christianity as wish-fulfilment and obsessional neurosis, but is blandly unaware that the same arguments could be applied to his own pan-sexual theory of psychoanalysis. Could it not be that this is an illusion? Did Freud not suffer an obsessional neurosis about sex? Such a criticism goes near the bone. It has been advanced by many serious psychologists. How about 'the beginnings of art, religion, ethics and society all meet in the Oedipus complex' as a piece of obsessional nonsense? Yet this was Freud's fantastic claim in *Totem and Tabu.* Those who write off what they do not understand as illusory must not be surprised at the retort of *tu quoque.*

The illusion of a future

Freud himself suffered from two obsessional illusions. One was the omnicompetence of science; the other the omnicompetence of psychoanalysis. He lived, admittedly, in the early days of scientific optimism, when men had some grounds for believing that it would solve all human problems. In his attack on religion in *The Future of an Illusion* he wrote, 'Science is no illusion. But it would be an illusion to suppose that we could get anywhere else what it cannot give us.' What a hollow ring there is about those words after the things our generation has lived through. What a naïve hope, in view both of the diabolical weapons for destruction which scientific advance has equipped us with, and of the world problems such as race rioting, ever-increasing crime, and the selfish refusal of the 'haves' to deal realistically with the hunger problem of the 'have-nots'. These are not problems to which science holds the key; selfish human nature is to blame for their threatening menace, and selfish human nature is not transformed into love by any scientific process. H. W. Puner in her book *Freud* made this comment on his scientific optimism: 'Thus one of the world's most determined disillusionists falls into the trap of ruthlessly tearing from life one of man's great illusions (*i.e.* religion), only to substitute another.' Freud may have suspected as much when, in his later years, jack-booted Nazis, following his own materialistic and determinist principles (though utterly devoid of his personal courtesy and kindness) kicked him out of house and home in Vienna, and sent him packing as a refugee to England. Even if he did not recognize the extent of his miscalculation, some of his most acute admirers did. Theodor Reik, in his book *From Thirty Years with Freud*, trenchantly criticized this hope of a religionless scientific Utopia as 'the illusion of a future'.

The limitations of psychoanalysis

If scientific optimism was one of Freud's illusions, the infallibility of analysis was the other. The claims he made for it have been recognized by many psychologists since his day as an unconscious attempt to establish a new and rival religion. Curiously enough, this is precisely what has happened in Soviet Russia, with the cult of Lenin. Not only is his tomb a place of constant pilgrimage, where even tough Communists pause to cross themselves and pray, but there are notices posted up in Russian factories to encourage production, such as 'Lenin sees you', 'Work for Lenin'. Many of the world's iconoclasts are quite unconscious of the new god in whose name they slay the old. Freud certainly was. 'Because his concept of reality was so narrow,' wrote

H. L. Philp in *Freud and Religious Belief*, 'he attempted to explain too much in terms of wishful thinking; and his attempt was probably the functioning of his own wishful thinking—his wish to explain everything in terms of his child and idol, psychoanalysis.' Philp's book provides a careful critique of Freud's views on religion, and it is all the more valuable because its author, unlike Freud who knew no theology and little about the Bible, is both a practising psychologist (with a healthy respect for Freud's clinical work) and a Christian theologian. Nor is he an isolated case of a psychologist who is a practising Christian. There are plenty of them. H. C. Rümke, Professor of Psychology at Utrecht, was even more forth-right than Philp. In *The Psychology of Unbelief* he not only convincingly rebutted Freud's claim that religion is an illusion, but also gave good reasons for supposing that unbelief is a symptom of arrested development.

None of these men would want to belittle the value of analysis. But their essential point is this. Granted that psychoanalysis can bring out, under favourable cir-cumstances, the best that is in a patient, nevertheless it cannot supply anything extra to support weak persona-lities. Hear the distinguished psychiatrist Stafford Clark. 'Thrown back on himself he (the patient) finds no com-fort and no solace in this final attempt at self-sufficiency. This is the crisis in analysis, and within its own frame-work analysis has no answer. The patient, groping beyond himself for the final answer, cannot get it from the analyst; for the transference, even if it were sufficient, cannot be maintained for a lifetime . . . Where, then, can a man turn? If full self-awareness and self-realization are not by themselves enough, what is? As a psychiatrist I know of no answer to this question: as a man I can only say with all humility that I believe in God.'[2]

What, you may ask, is to be gained by quoting Stafford

[2] *Psychiatry Today*, p. 287.

Clark against Freud? If the one believes God is a reality and the other regards him as an illusion, what does that show? Merely that when making judgments about God, psychologists are giving their own opinion, not the findings of their science. Psychology can no more be used either to bolster up or to discredit Christianity than the physical sciences can. Like them, psychology is a descriptive, not a prescriptive discipline. It analyses the nature and origin of people's beliefs, but it cannot dogmatize upon their truth or falsity. This must be established by other means. Now it *may* be that Freud is right in supposing that the Christian belief in the fatherly love of God is a reversion to our childhood father image which we project into the empty heavens. On the other hand, it *may* be the case that there is a God, and that he is best described as Father; indeed, as Ephesians 3:15 asserts, all human fatherhood may derive from him. Let us try to discover which of these two answers is the true one by applying certain tests to the Christian claim that God is real, and that relationship with him is no illusion. There are three which seem appropriate.

Three tests of validity

The first is the test of history. Christianity, as we have repeatedly seen, is a historical religion. To dispose of it, you must first get rid of, or explain away, its Founder. And that is a very difficult thing to do. As we saw in chapter one, various theories have been propounded which attempt to explain Jesus as a myth, and these have very properly been decisively discarded. The demythologizing debate raging on the Continent since Bultmann's famous essay in 1941, *The New Testament and Mythology*, is too complex a subject to go into here; sufficient to say that it uses the word 'myth' in a highly sophisticated way that certainly does *not* mean 'untrue' or 'illusory'. Moreover neither Bultmann nor his followers made the mistake of joining hands with the Christ-myth school; they never denied the historical nature of Jesus of Nazareth. The folly of all attempts to get rid of this historical Jesus was long ago exposed by Sir James Frazer, author of *The Golden Bough*, though he was no friend to Christianity. 'The doubts which have been cast on the historical reality of Jesus are in my judgment unworthy of serious attention. Quite apart from the positive evidence of history, the origin of a great moral and religious reform is incredible without the personal existence of a great reformer. To dissolve the founder of Christianity into a myth is as absurd as to do the same with Mohammed, Luther or Calvin.'

But granted the historicity of Jesus, what are we to make of him? His impact on the world was no illusion; why, we even date our era from his birth. His life of love and integrity, of courage and insight, unparalleled in the annals of mankind, is no illusion. There is nothing illusory about his claims to share God's character and attributes in a unique way. These are either true or sheer megalomania. His death was real enough, on the rough gibbet of a Roman cross. You may, of course, say that the idea of his resurrection is illusory, but if you do, you must in all good conscience be able to suggest a credible alternative. This has never been done. But by all means have a shot. You must explain the rise of the Christian movement, with nothing distinctive about it apart from the disciples' conviction that in Jesus crucified and risen they had the key to the meaning of life, to the character of God, to the destiny of believers. You must explain why Jesus's dispirited followers suddenly came to believe in his resurrection so passionately that they were prepared to confront hostile authorities, threatening crowds and death itself in the assurance that he was alive and with them still. There will be other little problems that require looking into: the empty tomb, the change of the day of rest from Saturday to Sunday, the amazing spread of the church, and, of course, the very existence of Christianity at all, not to mention the creation of the New Testament! In short, there is no lack of evidence about Jesus of Nazareth, upon whom the Christian religion is fairly and squarely based. The idea that Christianity is wish-fulfilment or self-delusion is shipwrecked on the solid rock of history.

The second test of the validity of Christian experience is character. Wherever this faith has appeared across the world and down the ages it has had notable effects upon those who practised it. It has made the immoral chaste, the greedy generous, the selfish loving, the cheat honest. It would be remarkable if an illusion produced this effect occasionally; but when you find the same effects constantly produced in prince and peasant, black and white, learned and illiterate, then you have every reason to regard this change as something real. An interesting testimony to this transformation of character brought about by the Christian faith is given by Charles Darwin. Commending the work of one Mr Fegan, a preacher in his own village, Darwin said, 'Your services have done more for the village in a few months than all our efforts for many years. We have never been able to reclaim a single drunkard, but through your services I do not know that there is a drunkard left in the village!' I heard only the other day of a striking example of the changed character the Christian faith creates. An engineer friend of mine told me, 'I have just met a woman of about thirty. Just over a week previously she had been a main-line heroin addict practising prostitution in one of our big cities. She had four children, all by different men, and suffered from severe psychological problems. One night she was walking the streets. Seeing the bright lights of a new coffee bar she went in. It so happened that this was run by a Christian group, and soon a clergyman was sitting alongside her listening to her pouring out her story. As a result she was brought to the special house for drug addicts where I met her.

'Looking at her now across the room it was hard to imagine what her past life had consisted of. There was a sparkle in her eyes, a gloss in her hair, a laugh on her lips. Only the thin, drawn look on her features revealed a hint of her past. She was already a new woman. And this came home to me all the more clearly when we started to pray for others in trouble. The simple direct way in which she spoke to God, thanking him, praising him, and asking him to touch the lives of others as he had hers, were all proof positive to me of the wonderful healing and integration of that woman, brought about by the Christian gospel. She was now a living testimony to God's love and power.'

This woman's story leads in naturally to the third test of the validity of religious experience, the test of power. All that we know about delusions suggests that they tend towards disintegration of character, unbalanced behaviour, and either the inability to achieve one's aims, or else the dissipation of energy in some strange byway of living. But Christianity has precisely the opposite effect. It makes men whole. I think of a razor-gang boy, converted suddenly one night when he drifted casually into a mission hall and now a happy and effective clergyman in Liverpool. I think of a lad who left school at 15 having achieved nothing, and shortly afterwards found faith in Christ. His life was revolutionized. He taught himself French, while serving in the Army. He passed successive stages of exams, collected an Honours B.D. while preparing for the ministry, and is now training others for ordination while he works for a doctorate in his spare time. He is as balanced and as useful in coffee-bar evangelism as he is in academic New Testament teaching, and his home is a joy to behold. His faith has integrated his whole personality. You would find it very difficult to persuade George that his Christianity is an illusion.

T. R. Glover once wrote, 'The strength of Christian convictions is measured by the forces of disruption and decline they have resisted.' True words, as one reflects on the persecutions, the changing ideologies, the cynicism from without and decay from within that have beset Christianity down the course of the last nineteen hundred years. For an illusion it is remarkably persistent.

Most illusions fade at the approach of death. If Christianity were indeed illusory, one would not expect it to stand up very well to this final test. But it does. History has shown repeatedly that 'our men die well'. Of course they do. They are convinced that death is a defeated enemy. They are confident that because their Master rose, they will share his life. Having lived with him and loved him during their lives, the fear of death does not unduly chill them. Perfect love casts out fear. Take the letter Hermann Lange wrote from his prison cell just before being executed for his faith by the Nazis. It is quoted, along with many others, in Trevor Huddleston's book *Dying We Live*. Lange tells his parents that two feelings occupied his mind the evening before he was to die. The death he had faced for so many months was now imminent. 'I am, first, in a joyous mood,' he wrote, 'and second, filled with great anticipation.' The joy came from 'faith in Christ who has preceded us in death. In him I have put my faith, and precisely today I have faith in him more firmly than ever.' He advised them to turn to the New Testament for consolation. 'Look where you will, everywhere you will find jubilation over the grace that makes us children of God. What can befall a child of God? Of what should I be afraid? On the contrary, rejoice!'

This victory over fear, especially fear of the ultimate horror, death, is one of the great moral triumphs of Christianity. It is quite inexplicable on the theory of illusion or auto-suggestion. 'By all psychological law', wrote Dr Crighton Miller, himself a distinguished psychoanalyst, 'the auto-suggestion of fear should be the strongest of all . . . unless some factor other than auto-suggestion is at work on the side of fearlessness.' Christ, I suggest, is that other factor on the side of fearlessness. He is real. He is alive. He is able to help, control and empower the Christian throughout his life right up to the end . . . and beyond it. That has always been the Christian message. It has been tested by the experience of millions. It is no illusion. But you will never experience it for yourself until you come to put your faith in the risen Jesus, whom you cannot see but for whose existence there is such strong evidence. When you take the momentous step of asking him to accept you, to come and take control of your life, then you will begin to find the reality of the claims the Christians make for their Lord. Then you will discover that Christianity is not an illusion, not an obsessional neurosis, but the key to life at its best.

CHAPTER FOUR

RUNNING AWAY FROM ADVENTURE

A conformist church

THE DISTINGUISHED Ghanaian sociologist, Dr K. Busia, gives some interesting material on the views about organized Christianity held by the majority of his sample in Birmingham. His book *Urban Churches in Britain* shows that common complaints were as follows. 'The church speaks mumbo-jumbo—not to, but over people.' 'They are upper class: not my kind.' 'They are so awfully dull. They never seem to do anything exciting.' Those three complaints, of the class structure, the inward orientation, and the dullness of the church are often repeated, and must be taken very seriously indeed. Perhaps the most damning of the three, not least in the mind of young people, is the third. Christianity is dull, solid, respectable. It is the Establishment.

It is in many ways a misfortune to have belonged to a culture, Western Christendom, which has been dominated by the church. In Britain, moreover, the church is 'by law established' and there are advantages in its close association with the State. But this can hardly be calculated to endear it to the young man full of reforming zeal, radical ideas, and a disposition to react against all that is old, conventional and dull.

This estimate of Christianity may also be due to the fact that, in Britain at least, a revolution in churchgoing habits has gone on during the past thirty years or so. It is almost certainly true that there has been a decline in real Christian belief and devotion since the end of the nineteenth century. But for the first generation of the twentieth century Christian standards were desired for society as a whole, and these were backed up with occasional churchgoing by the older generation, themselves very often the children of believing (and maybe narrow) Christian homes. But the churchgoing did not mean a great deal to them. It was just one of the things that was 'done' by that generation. It is an engaging example of the Englishman's unwillingness to be extreme in any respect, that in the years up to the Second World War it was deemed socially improper not to go to church at all; but it was thought equally surprising and quaint if one went too often!

The children of this generation of occasional churchgoers are the young people of the sixties. Quite apart from the natural battle between the generations, which would lead the teenager to reject church if his Dad went, there is an additional reason for the present reaction. Very often 'Dad', if he was the typical Englishman of this period, remained entirely unchanged by his religion. It made not the least difference to the way he behaved on Monday whether or not he had been to church on Sunday. His visits to church did not influence his business ethics or make him a more pleasant chap about the home. Is it surprising if the younger generation regards such churchgoing as hypocritical?

Harold Loukes collected some characteristic attitudes of young people to religion in his revealing paperback *Teenage Religion*. The shrewdness of their exposure of mere churchianity needs no underlining. 'Every church has the same atmosphere—a dead atmosphere', said one. Another saw through the merely conventional religiosity of his father's generation: 'The main body of the congregation nowadays goes to church because "it's good for you", not because they are religious.' A third thought most churchgoers were out to stock up some capital in the bank of heaven: 'You find nearly all old people going to church because I think they want to get on the good side of God before they die.'

This attitude of rebellion against the conformity of churchgoing is to be found throughout the whole kaleidoscope of society. It is even there in the public schools, those bastions of the Establishment, where agnosticism is now fashionable, compulsory chapel on the way out, the Bishop of Woolwich a hero. This is not, I discover, because they read his books, much less understand them; but because the Bishop represents that rarity on the episcopal bench, a man who is against the Establishment, an adventurous thinker, a true radical. What could be more calculated to endear him to the youthful heart? What, incidentally, could indicate more clearly the view of Christianity held by those boys, that it is merely an institution which props up the *status quo*?

A revolutionary movement

This view would have astounded the early Christians. They belonged to a burning revolutionary movement, headed by the most adventurous and challenging of leaders. It is a terrible indictment of the church that it has succeeded in giving the impression that somehow Jesus was a gentle, orthodox figure, on the side of bourgeois values, faintly defensive and somewhat conservative. We have tamed Jesus, fossilized him, imprisoned him inside conventional churches and institutional religion. This is a crying shame. It is a slander on Jesus Christ, and it is the precise opposite of the spirit he intended to instil in his followers.

What has happened, I think, is this. Some people's religion is indeed, as we saw in the last chapter, a form of escapism. It is soft and feckless, rather than tough and adventurous. And much of what goes on in the churches feeds such an attitude. Many of the hymns that we sing, 'Art thou weary, art thou languid, art thou sore distressed? . . .', 'There is a blessèd home beyond this land of woe . . .', 'Abide with me . . .', 'Brief life is here our portion . . .', 'Jerusalem, my happy home . . .' are scarcely exciting; they look forward to a state of passive bliss. The very absence of challenge in the hymns the churches sing and the things the churches do is eloquent explanation for the shortage of teenagers in those same churches.

Freud was perfectly right in asserting that all men oscillate between the death urge and the life urge. One has only to reflect on the conflicting emotions that arise in the mind when it is time to get up on a cold winter morning to appreciate his point! What many churches have failed to realize is that in the teens and twenties the life urge very much predominates over the other. Christianity ought, accordingly, to be presented in terms of the challenge, the ideal, the adventure of making the very most out of life by putting the maximum into it. Instead, we find it presented in terms of the death urge, with the accent on duty, on conformity to accepted patterns of behaviour and speech, on sitting silent while the clergyman preaches and prays, on the comforts of the life to come, on the wisdom of sitting loose to the things of time and space! Is it any wonder that this makes little appeal to full-blooded young people? Is it any wonder they think Christianity dull and boring as well as useless?

A radical leader

But the death urge is certainly not the main emphasis in Christianity. It is part of the Christian message, sure enough: for Christianity claims to be relevant to a man from the cradle to the grave. There is, therefore, room for understanding Jesus as gentle, meek and mild. There is room for dwelling on the everlasting arms which encompass the dying man. But that is not the main note struck by the teaching of Jesus nor by the activities of the first Christians. Jesus was as adventurous as any radical in his teaching and in his attitudes to life. His most scathing assault was on the priests whose vested interest was to keep the people 'a little civilized by religion'. He was the avowed enemy of that religion which was the opiate of the people, and of the religious men who prepared the prescription.

It is not too much to see parallels between official religion in his day and in our own. It was on the side of political and economic conservatism: the traditions of the past must not be broken, the Roman occupying forces must not be annoyed. He split wide open this canny attitude. On the *economic* side, the Jews of his day believed that material prosperity was the signal mark of God's blessing on a man. Yet Jesus was penniless, and apparently was content to be so. He warned men not to lay up for themselves ephemeral treasure on earth, but to be rich towards God, rich in love, in faith, in mercy and prayer. He instanced the rich fool, who thought he could gain lasting satisfaction from money—until the night when the God who gave him life took it back again, and he lost all that he had lived for. He told men it was more happy to give than to get: what was that if not a revolutionary attitude towards wealth? Jesus of Nazareth can hardly be accused of being on the side of the financial *status quo*. And if some of his followers have been, it is the measure of their disobedience to their Master.

What of the *social* conservatism inculcated by contemporary Jewish religion? The typical rabbi was convinced of the superiority first of the Jews to all others, then of the Pharisees to all Jews, then of the Jewish male to all women. The punctilious religious leaders, so careful to wash ceremonially before meals, and to tithe even their garden produce, despised the *am ha-aretz*, 'the people of the land', who could never aspire to saintliness:

they had neither the time nor the learning to carry out the religious niceties of their mentors. The Pharisees looked down on them. They despised the common people, the women and children, and most of all the Gentile 'dogs'. Judaism was as caste-ridden as Hinduism.

But Jesus would have none of this. He ate with the outcasts as freely as he did with the Pharisees. He was as concerned for women and children, lepers and the mentally deranged as he was for learned lawyers and revered priests. He had no time for formalism and hypocrisy, for washing ceremoniously before dinner or wearing special clothes to eat it. He refused to fast from habit or for effect; but only when need arose in the service of God or men. He taught that it made no difference where you worshipped God so long as your heart was right in his sight. He saw more faith in a Gentile officer than in the 'brood of vipers' which constituted the Pharisaic clergy. Hardly a social conformist in matters of religion! That is why the top people hated him so much. That, in the last analysis, is why they hounded him to death. He was much too uncomfortable a nonconformist to live with. Either he must go or they must.

So far from being a tame conservative, Jesus of Nazareth was a peaceful though highly adventurous revolutionary; he was a radical to his fingertips. We shall consider five aspects of his very novel and demanding teaching.

Novel teaching about God

First-century Judaism had domesticated the Almighty. He had been cut down to a comfortable size. He remained the God of the whole earth in theory, no doubt; but in practice he was merely the God of Israel. Jews thought of Israel as God's son and the Gentiles as outsiders, dogs, sons of the devil. Jesus calmly reversed this estimate! So far from being sons of God by virtue of their descent from

Abraham, some at least of the Jews made it plain by their attitudes and actions that the devil was their father. Jesus argued (in John 8) that if they were, as they proudly claimed, sons of God, they would listen to him, for he had come to give them the fullest possible revelation of the heavenly Father. Instead, they plotted to kill him. In so doing, Jesus pointed out, they were showing their parentage from the devil who was a murderer from the beginning. In ways like this Jesus brought home to his hearers the unwelcome truth that the devil had got just as firm a grip of Israel, the Chosen People, as he had of the Gentile world.

But once he had dispelled this hard-dying illusion (as frequently met with among educated people of the twentieth century as it was among religious Jews of the first) that all men are sons of God, Jesus went on to show that God was so gracious, so loving and merciful that he was longing to accept all and sundry into his family. God does not write off the lost sheep, the lost coin, the lost son. He cares so much for them that he goes out to seek them. That is the indelible picture of God which Jesus gave to the world.

On more than one occasion Jesus pictured God as throwing a party, in which he made full and generous provision for all who would come. The respectable and self-righteous turned down the invitation to this great feast, while the folk who knew that they were utterly unqualified poured in with glad amazement. Is that not a wonderfully adventurous picture of God, as one who is prepared to accept all who are not too proud to come? Is it not a wonderfully adventurous picture of Christianity? No matter of dull virtue or precise ceremonial, but a great supper, a party? That may be a surprising conception of the Christian faith; shame on the churches if so. But it is unquestionably the true reflection of the teaching of Jesus. The God he revealed cares for men, comes to find them in their lostness, and satisfies them once he has found them. That is the Christian God. And any assessment of Christianity which does not come to terms with this description of God is not adventurous enough; it is too cramped, too dull, too conservative.

Searching assessment of man

Jesus was no less fresh and challenging in his teaching about man. Two opposite estimates of human value were current in his day, as indeed they still are today. Jesus rejected both.

One tendency was to depersonalize man. Life was cheap in the first century. The sick, the aged, the outcast: people shrugged their shoulders. But Jesus affirmed the dignity of man. Mankind was made by God, loved by God, sustained by God. A man was of more value than many sparrows, though the heavenly Father was concerned for them too. We have seen in chapter two how Jesus asserted the value of man and acted on it in his every attitude to other people. He was concerned to help the poor, the underprivileged, the diseased. They mattered very much to him – just as much as the well-to-do, the religious and the important. That was radical teaching and practice in those days, and it is adventurous enough today, when in the West bigger and bigger mergers tend to reduce man to a mere cog in the economic machine, while in the East totalitarian ideologies reduce him to a pawn in the political and social scene.

But if Jesus protested vehemently against the current devaluation of man, he was just as strongly opposed to the tendency which had come into Judaism from the Greek world, to glorify man, to regard him as the measure of all things, almost to deify him. Jesus saw man as a temple, to be sure, but a ruined temple. Quick though he was to notice and commend the good in his fellow men, he nevertheless unveiled, as nobody had done so devastatingly before him, the latent possibilities for evil within human nature. It came out quite casually in phrases such as, 'If you then, who are evil, know how to give good gifts to your children.' It emerged in stories such as the son who deliberately left his father's home and then ran away to waste his life with corrupt companions in a foreign country. It blazed out in his scorching denunciations of men's false motives when praying, fasting or giving to God. It appeared, with breath-taking candour, in his condemnation of the lustful look as the source of adultery, or the bitter word as the origin of murder.

This realistic assessment of the weaknesses of human nature stands out in startling contrast to the starry-eyed optimism about man's loving heart and golden future which was current then as now in progressive circles. A few years ago I was struck by the naïvety of the Annual Report of the then Metropolitan Commissioner of Police to the Home Secretary. He wrote, 'The most distressing feature in the rise of crime today is that neither the absence of real poverty, nor the progress in methods of dealing with delinquents have done anything to reduce the volume.' The *Daily Telegraph*, commenting on this Report, admitted that it, too, was baffled by the increase in crime, now that poverty, once almost universally adduced as its chief cause, has almost disappeared. But there would have been no need to be baffled, were we not so drunk with the achievements of mankind, particularly in the technical sphere, that we have become blind to the truth, so clearly taught by Jesus, that evil deeds have their root in the human heart, and that the varied troubles of our world all proceed, in the last analysis, from inside human nature.

Such was Jesus's remarkable assessment of mankind. Man is not junk—he is made in the image of God, and matters to God. Neither is man divine—he has within him the seeds of every variety of evil. In setting such a high value on man, yet penetrating so shrewdly to the source of his weaknesses, Jesus gave an unconventional and unpopular but highly realistic evaluation of the human scene. We have only to look at the daily newspaper (if introspection is too painful) to be convinced of its truth.

Staggering personal claims

Jesus is unique among the teachers of the world in that he had so much to say about himself. Others taught extensively about God, but did not make extravagant claims about themselves. Mohammed might say, 'Allah is one, and Mohammed is his prophet', but he never laid claim to anything approaching deity. The same might be said of Confucius or Buddha. But this is just where Jesus Christ is so different. He did not conform to the normal pattern among religious leaders of teaching some new thing about God, or way to God. He dared to assert, 'No one knows the Son but the Father, and no one knows the Father but the Son and those to whom the Son may choose to reveal him' (Matthew 11:27). What a fantastic claim! It is very similar to that in John 10:1, 9, 'In truth I tell you, in very truth, the man who does not enter the sheepfold by the door, but climbs in some other way, is nothing but a thief or a robber . . . I am the door; anyone who comes into the fold through me shall be safe.' Jesus laid claim to be the way to God in person.

What is more, he asserted that he had a relationship with God which no-one had ever claimed before. It comes out in the Aramaic word *Abba* which he was so fond of using, especially in prayer. Nobody before him in all the history of Israel had addressed God by this word. For it is the intimate, family word that a child might use of his Daddy. To be sure, Jews were accustomed to praying to God as Father: but the word they used was *Abhinu*, a form of address which was essentially an appeal to God for mercy and forgiveness. There is no appeal to God for mercy in Jesus's mode of address, *Abba*. It is the familiar word of closest intimacy. That is why he differentiated between his own relationship with God as Father and that of other people. He never said 'Our Father', aligning himself with his disciples, but rather referred to 'My God and your God, my Father and your Father'. He was Son of God in a quite different sense from other men who were merely God's creation. This word *Abba* was the heart of the good news he had come to bring; it told that he had a unique filial relationship with God, and was prepared to share it with the utterly unworthy, if they committed themselves to him. Professor Jeremias, commenting on this remarkable word in *The Central Message of the New Testament*, summed up its significance in these words: 'Here was the man who had the power to address God as *Abba*, and who included publicans and sinners in the Kingdom by authorising them to repeat this one word, "*Abba*, Father".'

The passage of time from the first century until now has dulled the sense of shock that claims like this must have made on his contemporaries. Nothing like them had ever been heard before; nor has it since, for that matter, outside the walls of a madhouse. Here was a Jewish peasant teacher saying in sober, earnest tones, I give men eternal life, and they shall never perish; 'no one shall snatch them from my care. My Father who has given them to me is greater than all, and no one can snatch them out of the Father's care. *My Father and I are one*' (John 10:28–30). He told a puzzled disciple, 'Anyone who has seen me has seen the Father' (John 14:9). John later explains the relationship of Jesus to his

Father as that of a word to a mind, the form the unseen intelligence takes in self-expression (John 1:1). The writer to the Hebrews put it memorably when he said that Jesus, the Son, corresponded as closely to the Father as radiance to the sun, or as the impression to the seal (Hebrews 1:2). Jesus laid claim to nothing less than sharing God's essential and eternal nature when he said, 'Before Abraham was born, I am' (John 8:58; see Exodus 3:14 for the background to the phrase). There is no getting away from the greatness of the claim Jesus made here. It cannot be watered down. The Jews were themselves well aware of this, and tried to stone him out of hand for blasphemy. It was the same when he defended his Sabbath activities by saying that his Father was ceaselessly at work. 'This made the Jews still more determined to kill him, because he was not only breaking the Sabbath, but, by calling God his own Father, he claimed equality with God' (John 5:18).

Such were the breathtaking claims of this unique man. He told the Jews, not that God would judge them at the Last Day, but that he had committed all judgment to the Son (John 5:27). He called on his hearers not to return to God, but to come to him (Matthew 11:28). He did not proclaim, like the Buddha, 'This is the way: follow it', but 'I am the way' and 'follow me' (John 14:6; Mark 1:17). He did not promise that God would eventually pardon, but he proclaimed forgiveness here and now on his own authority, 'Son, your sins *are* forgiven' (Mark 2:5). Wherever you look in the Gospels or, for that matter, any of the early Christian writings, the claim is the same. It is put in different ways in different books. The first three Gospels express it in a different way from St John. But the inescapable point remains: Jesus Christ is the centre of his own message. He, and he alone, can bring men to God; because he, and he alone, brings God to men.

The claims considered

Now when considering the validity of these claims, several points must be borne in mind. First, the context of such assertions. They were made before the most hostile audience imaginable. Nowhere else in the Mediterranean world of the day did you find an exclusive monotheism. The Jews were ridiculed for it, albeit humoured in it by their Roman overlords. But at least they stuck firmly to it. Over centuries they had slowly and painfully learned this lesson, that there is but one God, the God of the whole earth; he had chosen to disclose himself to Israel, and Israel accordingly refused to tolerate any image of God, let alone any person making divine claims. So monotheistic were they that when an indiscreet Roman governor entered Jerusalem with his legionary standards (bedecked with a few medallions with images on them) there was a riot, and the governor, Pontius Pilate, was angrily cautioned for his provocation by the Emperor Tiberius.

That was the climate in which Jesus set about claiming nothing less than deity. And what is more, he got men to believe it. Lots of men. Not just the simple fisher folk of Galilee, but shrewd tax men, intelligent scholars, a whole company of priests, and even, after a time, members of his own family. It is a sobering thought that the Christian movement which makes these extreme claims for Jesus arose in the most inimical soil possible, the hard ground of monotheistic Jewry. All the earliest converts to Christianity who came to acknowledge that 'Jesus is Lord' (and 'Lord' was the name for God himself in the Old Testament) were Jews! That is a fact which requires some explanation if one is disposed to reject the claims of Jesus about himself.

Second, consider the author of these claims. He was a very humble, modest man, a peasant teacher who sought no honour for himself. He liked ordinary people, particularly the downtrodden and underprivileged, the poor and sick. He was a friend, no less, of tax gatherers and the most unrespectable members of society. There was no suspicion of pride about him. Indeed, he exposed it ruthlessly in others. It is, of course, possible that he was mad, so taken up with his own importance that he suffered from a form of megalomania. That is not unknown. Hitler had it; so, probably, did Napoleon. But it is an exceedingly implausible explanation once you take the total character of Jesus into account: his balance, his sanity, his ethical teaching, his self-sacrifice, his love, his concern for others. Very few people have ever read the Gospels honestly and come away saying 'The man is mad'. Such a conclusion savours too much of running away from an uncomfortable truth that Jesus was what he claimed to be. C. S. Lewis disposed of it succinctly. 'The discrepancy', he wrote in *Miracles*, 'between the depth and sanity, and (let me add) *shrewdness* of his moral teaching, and the rampant megalomania which must lie behind his theological teaching unless he is indeed God, has never been satisfactorily got over.'

Third, it is worth remembering the impact of those claims of his. Men were unable to resist the challenge they brought; they found themselves driven into one of two camps. We do not find people praising Jesus in the Gospel story; we do not find them commending him. Either they responded to Jesus with the love and devotion they would accord to God himself, or else they tried to kill him. They did not say, as many who have run away from this evidence and tried to evade the dilemma have said, 'Jesus Christ was the best of men'. That is an assessment which nobody at the time seems to have made about him. They were either for him, as Son of God, or else violently against him.

Sometimes the very act of killing a man is a form of

escapism. In this case it certainly was. They could not bear his teaching and his character, and so they hounded him to death. Imagine the situation. The Jewish religious leaders had been publicly exposed by the teaching of this unordained peasant. (If you want to see the extent of those denunciations, read Matthew 23.) They were not, we may be sure, grateful for such painful home truths. They did not cherish loving thoughts towards him in their hearts. If they had known of any piece of mud that they could have thrown at him and made it stick, they would gladly have hurled it. Indeed, we know they did – at his trial. But even so, their accusations would not agree in detail; the mud did not stick. When Jesus asked an infuriated crowd, infuriated because he had claimed equality with God, 'Which of you convicts me of sin?' there was no reply. How acutely irritating for his opponents to be rendered speechless! So they ran away from the implication of his sinlessness (that he might, after all, be claiming no more than the sober truth) and determined to rid themselves of his uncomfortable presence by killing him. An entirely understandable and utterly conformist reaction to the radical claims of Jesus.

New light on death, in theory and practice

Our tame, mollycoddled society has come to regard death as the greatest of all misfortunes that could happen to a man; something to be deferred as long as possible, then to be glossed over with soothing periphrases. We are not only afraid of meeting death, we are afraid of talking honestly about it. It is the forbidden subject of conversation in today's runaway world.

There is a most striking contrast to all this in the teaching and attitude of Jesus. He did not see death as the greatest disaster that could happen to a man. Far from it. Because he knew death was not the end, he taught men that there were circumstances in which it was preferable to continued life on earth. He called those happy who were willing to be persecuted and killed for their testimony to him and the good news of the salvation he had brought for men. But he went further. He said that death was the only gateway to life in any sphere. Just as the seed of wheat was useless unless it fell into the ground and 'died', so it was with a man's ego, his character, his existence. Jesus enunciated the profound paradox that if you hold on to your life and your possessions, you will inevitably lose them; if you renounce them, you will find a new liberty, a new life opening up.

It is all very well to talk like that. Several of the world's great leaders have done the same. But did Jesus carry it out in practice? Actually, his behaviour in this matter was even more adventurous and radical than his precept. Jesus died as a young man in the prime of life. He died one of the most agonizing deaths man's inhumanity to man has ever devised. He died voluntarily: there was no need for him to venture back into the lion's mouth at Jerusalem, where the massed echelons of his religious antagonists were just waiting for him. But he 'set his face resolutely towards Jerusalem'. He told his puzzled followers that, like the good shepherd, he would lay down his life for the sheep: 'No one takes it from me, but I lay it down of my own accord.' This is heroism indeed, but it is not the half of what Jesus did. He had lived with this shadow over his life for years, almost throughout his public ministry. We read early on in Mark's account how the nationalistic Pharisees and the quisling supporters of the puppet king Herod had made an unnatural alliance to eradicate Jesus (Mark 3:6). This is entirely credible. Jesus had embarked on a collision course with officialdom. Only one outcome was possible, and he knew it well. Yet he continued with his wonderful teaching, his gracious work of healing and love, utterly unconcerned about himself and totally at the disposal of others.

Even this was not all. Time after time in the Gospels we find him forecasting with remarkable precision the death he would die. In a sense this was not too difficult a piece of foresight; rejection by the rulers would inevitably lead to a capital charge before the occupying Roman power, and when the Romans executed a lower-class native of an occupied country they crucified him, after scourging him first. Jesus would not have needed even to be a prophet to anticipate this much of his fate.

The really remarkable thing is the interpretation he gave to his death. He said that he would 'give his life as a ransom for many' (Mark 10:45). He was using evocative language full of meaning both to Greek and Jew. The word 'ransom' had long been associated with the freeing of slaves in the ancient Greek world. A slave was set free for ever once a costly price had been paid by some benefactor. His death, Jesus suggested, was that costly price which would win liberation from the slavery to wrongdoing which shackles the will of Everyman. That word 'ransom' meant even more to the Jew. It cast his mind back to the rescue from Egypt which constituted Israel as a nation. They were liberated from bondage and death in Egypt on the night of Passover. The twelfth chapter of Exodus recounts the story. Each household in Israel escaped the destruction which befell all the first-born in Egypt by killing a lamb and painting its blood above the door of their houses. The death of the lamb, coupled with reliance on its efficacy, saved the Jews on that historic night, and they left Egypt for ever, on their way to Canaan, the land of life and liberty. Jesus was using language associated with that crucial event in Israel's history when he spoke of his death as a ransom.

However, as the prophets had so clearly seen, Israel

was still the victim of evil and wickedness within, although she had been rescued from the external domination of Egypt. What she needed was someone to ransom her from her sins. This need gave rise to one of the most sublime poems in all literature, Isaiah 53, in which the suffering Servant of God, himself utterly righteous and sinless, voluntarily bears the sin of many in order that they may be put in the right with God. He identifies himself with what they are, in order that they may share what he is. That, Jesus declared, was the destiny he had come to fulfil. Innocent and perfect as he was, he proposed to identify himself with the evil of men, taking responsibility for it in his own person, so that they could share his own status and character before God. It is the very principle of life through death which he had stressed in his teaching. But it is even more wonderful than that: for it is *our* life through *his* death. The whole Bible makes it clear that man's rebellion against God has very serious effects. It cuts us off from enjoying life with God, and nothing we do can right this situation. But what nobody can do for himself or for another, God himself has done for us all—such is the meaning of Christ's death. Jesus has restored the broken communications between mankind and God, though it cost him his own life to do so. He tasted the God-forsakenness proper to men who had deliberately forsaken God, when he cried on the cross, 'My God, my God, why hast thou forsaken me?' He took responsibility for the sheer wickedness of men so that we might go free. He died, that we might live. What fantastic courage! It brought from the lips of Paul the wondering cry of amazement, 'Christ Jesus came into the world to save *sinners*. And I am the foremost of sinners.'

Could Jesus have done anything more superb than that? Anything more appropriate to our deepest need? Because he dealt once and for all on the cross with the fundamental issue of man's relationship to God, we can face our Maker and our Judge unafraid: provided, that is, we have enlisted in the ranks of Jesus.

New horizons to living

The urge to live is the deepest of our instincts. We not only hang on to life, we want to wring the last drop of excitement out of it. We all have our different recipes for making the most of life—success, respectability, influence over other people, money, and so forth. None of them can be said to be an unqualified success, if one may judge by the number of dissatisfied people one meets. What is more, the real enjoyment we do derive from our chosen pursuits is often spoiled by fear, loneliness, worry, disappointment or sheer beastliness (our own or other people's). Despite all our enthusiasm about living, we have not yet found the key to a really satisfying life. Jesus, on the other hand, does seem to have possessed that secret. The records we have of his life are unanimous in presenting us with a picture of a man who was always at peace, always happy in the relationship of love he enjoyed with his heavenly Father, always concerned for the well-being of others, always in control of himself, never lonely even when alone, never worried even in a crisis. It is a life which has haunted the greatest artists and the most profound thinkers from his day to our own. If he had said something about what makes life really satisfying, it would be well worth paying attention to.

In fact, he has said a great deal about this subject. Nowhere did he put it more succinctly than in a prayer of his recorded in John 17:3: 'This is eternal life: to know thee who alone art truly God, and Jesus Christ whom thou hast sent.' Those words strike a note which is both familiar and unfamiliar. On the one hand Jesus is saying that the key to living is meeting; that personal relationships are the most important and satisfying things in life—the meeting of two minds, the friendship of two colleagues, the love of man for woman, the devotion of parents to children. That makes sense and it is not new. But the shattering, new thing that Jesus is asserting is this. Personal relationships must include God if they are to be lived to the full. So far from making life dull and crabbed, a living relationship with his Creator makes a man's life free and wonderful.

There is much talk these days of God being dead. The god who used to plug the gaps in our scientific knowledge is certainly dead. The comfortable benevolent god who took all decent middle-class Englishmen to heaven but was not too fussy about the rest is dead too. The god of 'church on Sunday and live as you please the rest of the week' is dead. And a good thing too. But the One who is the source both of the universe and human personality, who is the sum of all that is good and beautiful and true, this God is not dead. He is the living God, and he is concerned for us. He made us. He sustains us. He loves us— so much that he wants to come and share life with us. And when that happens, a new dimension is added to living. Jesus called it 'eternal life' in order to emphasize not so much its duration as its quality. How is it possible, we may wonder, to 'know thee who alone art truly God' in this sense of personal relationship? The answer lies in 'Jesus Christ whom thou hast sent'.

Jesus lived a full, adventurous, supremely happy life. He surrendered this life on the cross, freely and vicariously for us, as we saw above. But that was not the end of the matter. During his ministry Jesus had repeatedly forecast that he would rise from the dead (see, *e.g.*, Mark 8:31; 9:31; 10:34). He was as good as his word. He did rise from the dead. The evidence in favour of this astonishing fact is overwhelming. If you wish to see a journalist's scrutiny of it, read Frank Morison's *Who Moved the Stone?* Professor J. N. D. Anderson's *The*

Evidence for the Resurrection gives the approach of a leading lawyer to the evidence, which he regards as utterly compelling; a thoughtful theologian's study is provided by Archbishop A. M. Ramsey's *The Resurrection of Christ*.

Jesus rose triumphant from that cold tomb of death. God raised him, partly in order to vindicate his claims to deity (see Romans 1:4, 'declared Son of God by a mighty act in that he rose from the dead'), partly in order to show that he had been victorious in his battle with the very root forces of evil and having borne the worst that evil could do to him, had emerged alive, as the compelling proof that wickedness will not have the final word in God's world. But one of the most important purposes of his resurrection was this: in order that he could share life with his followers anywhere in the world or down the centuries. A Christian is a man who has encountered the risen Christ and shares life with him. He is not someone who is following a dead leader, or trying to live by the Sermon on the Mount. No. He is someone in whose personality Christ has taken up residence by his Spirit. So fundamental is this that St Paul can say 'If a man does not possess the Spirit of Christ, he is no Christian'. It is this indwelling presence of Jesus Christ in their lives which makes new men of Christians. It is this which transforms their characters, and changes them, albeit slowly and laboriously, into likeness to Christ.

And of course, that is Christ's exciting answer to the problems of anxiety, fear, and so on which, as we saw, spoil our enjoyment of life. The Christian is not *lonely*, because he has with him the one who has promised 'Be assured, I am with you always, to the end of time'—and this makes an enormous difference in situations which would otherwise be unbearable. Men like Richard Wurmbrand testify to the presence of Christ with them in prison and torture for their faith, as the one factor which saved them from going out of their minds. The

Christian is not *disappointed*, because, although he gets his fair share of misfortune, 'we know that to those who love God, . . . everything that happens fits into a pattern for good' (Romans 8:28, Phillips). Whatever his circumstances, he learns contentment in them, for the logic of Hebrews 13:5 is irresistible: 'Be content with what you have; for God himself has said, "I will never leave you or desert you".' Nor does *worry* bite insidiously into the Christian's peace of mind. He shares his concerns with his ever-present Friend, and has learned the wisdom of St Peter's advice, 'Cast all your care upon him, for it matters to him about you.' Best of all, the weaknesses and sinfulness of the Christian's own nature are gradually healed by the Spirit of Christ: the fruit of that Spirit's presence is increasingly felt as 'love, joy, peace, long-suffering, gentleness' and the rest of those attractive qualities grow in the Christian's life. The things that deform our characters are progressively removed, and the Christian is free to live life to the full, as he was intended to, sharing his experiences every day and hour with his Maker, Redeemer and Indweller. If there is any answer to the deepest enigmas of life which is more radical, more exciting, more adventurous than that, I should like to hear of it. It is certainly not the genuine Christians who can be accused of running away from adventure. Is it not rather those conformists who are loath to commit themselves to such a 'high octane' quality of life?

Cowardly conformity

Such was the teaching, such the living of Jesus of Nazareth. To follow him is certainly costly; it will demand involvement, love, self-sacrifice. But it draws the best out of a man. Like all revolutionary leaders, Jesus offers blood, tears, toil, sweat. And as with Garibaldi and Churchill, men responded if they had the courage, if they possessed the spirit of adventure. Such a challenge touched off the spark of endurance, of risk, of initiative in them; they accepted the challenge, and they never regretted it.

It is worth reflecting on the type of people who first responded to Jesus. Few of the soft inhabitants of southern Palestine, few of the smug priests, few of the dignified rulers, few of the safe Establishment. It was the rough-tongued, wild-tempered men of Galilee who had the courage to follow him. He could do something with the life and energy, the impulsiveness and foolhardiness of these men, whereas he could do little with the tame decorum of the 'religious'. It is still the case today that the most dynamic Christians are usually those who have been won from atheism or apathy, in contrast to those who have always been brought up in church circles. For Christianity is the faith for men who are prepared to swim against the stream. It is the religion for radicals.

I believe there is a soft streak in many young people today. They are ready to poke fun at their friends who take their religion seriously, allowing it to make them generous and loving, self-sacrificing and pure. But they have not the courage to follow them. It is easier to stay on the side-lines and jeer. The magazine *Newsweek* devoted an entire issue in 1965 to the student generation; the conclusion it came to was that the students, on their own admission, although so radical in their talk, were depressingly conformist in their behaviour. They did not have the guts to be different. 'Flaming moderates', the Editor of *The New York Post* called them. Rebels without an ideology, they anticipated, quite rightly, that for all their audacious ideas, they would turn out just like their parents, worrying about the job, the mortgage, the children, social standing, and how to get out of the rut! What is true of the modern young American is no less true in other countries. I was speaking on this subject in a South African university, and after my talk a fine, strong, handsome young man asked if he might print my address in a student magazine. I looked him in the eyes and asked him what he was going to do about the adventure of aligning himself with so challenging a leader as Jesus Christ. His eyes fell, and he muttered, 'I haven't the guts'. He wanted to print the talk, but he shrank from getting involved.

This holds good for many people today. It is not that they don't believe or can't believe that the records about Jesus are true, or that he can make a great difference to those who trust him; many of them have friends who have become Christians and they have noticed the difference in them. It is really a matter of 'guts'. They haven't the courage to give themselves to a costly, demanding Christian programme: they prefer to remain on the side of the Establishment, pursuing economic and social security. It is surprising to find the absence of moral courage among people who are often physically very brave; but so it is. They would rather risk death in a moon probe than step out of line with their friends by doing anything different from the crowd. They lack the courage to live dangerously with Christ, instead of safe and sound with the rest. For discipleship can be dangerous; it can mean social ostracism, even persecution; and it can lead a man or woman with excellent prospects at home to give them all up in order to be of service to a developing country. It is altogether easier to avoid that sort of risk by sitting in the ranks of the agnostics (not the atheists, by the way: it is safer to be an agnostic, as one of the students interviewed in *Newsweek* admitted, just in case there might turn out to be a God after all!). I have found the lack of moral courage to be a notable characteristic both of the sixth-form and of the university opposition to Christianity which I have met. As one

Oxford friend wrote to his father about his friends, 'The problem with most of them, I discover, is not to convince them that Christianity is true; many are honest enough with themselves to admit they are convinced; yet they are not honest enough with themselves to act on what they believe.'

Costly adventure

Compare this craven attitude with the adventurous courage of a Sudanese Christian pastor whose news I recently received. This man has experienced cruel persecution from the soldiers of the North of the Sudan. The theological college of which he was a member was overrun in the middle of the night and was razed to the ground. Some of the students and staff were killed; others escaped into the bush. They had no possessions, no food apart from what they could gather in the forest. His wife gave birth to a child during their arduous trek to a neighbouring country.

Eventually this man came to England for a while, and we heard his story from his own lips. Was he discouraged? Did opposition and destitution cause him to lose his faith in God's love and goodness? Far from it. He found more joy in the adventure of sharing hardships with his Christian flock than in enjoying the comforts of conformist England. Back now in a part of the Congo adjoining Sudan, he is ministering to his exiled compatriots. He lives with fear: 'Our hearts were in fear at the troubles in the East of the Congo, because it was very close, and our fear was, "Can we enter again in the bush to hide ourselves?" . . . We at moment live in peace. We don't know what is going to happen tomorrow.' He lives with poverty: 'The Lord has been so kind to us in this country through friends. He has supplied our need, even though it means cutting out some of the things like breakfast, tea, lamp oil, yet we still praise him for his kindness.' But he lives with joy, joy at the presence of the Lord with him, and joy at the growth of the work of the Lord through him. 'The work of God among the Sudanese refugees scattered has gone very well, and many people have been baptised: for example in the area of — I baptised 409. In Congo as a whole almost in these past three years of refugee five thousand have been baptised. . . . Praise the Lord the church in Congo has been so friendly to us even though they are not of our society.'

The pressures on a white South African graduate I recently met are more subtle. She is a Jewess who has become a Christian. I gave something of her story in *Man Alive!* She has since written to tell me of her seventeen-year-old sister's conversion to Christ. 'My father won't allow her to go to any Christian meetings or church services at all. He won't even allow her to meet Christian friends of mine. The opposition is tremendous. He simply won't see reason at all. He can't realize that nothing he can do can stop her being a Christian.' Talking of her own experience in three years of Christian living she continues: 'I praise God for these years of joyful service. It hasn't been all plain sailing, but by far the biggest encouragement has been my sister's conversion. . . . A Jewish girl M— H— has also been converted, so it looks as though God is revealing himself to his own Jewish people. I can't wait to start working full time among my own people, telling them of their Messiah and Saviour. I spoke at a girls' school recently, and five Jewish girls came up to me afterwards.'

Such is the joy, such the toughness of following the adventurous programme of Jesus of Nazareth. I wonder how many of those who read these lines will have the courage to live as a Christian. Dare you rebel against the tacit rebellion against God in which you have been living, accept his free pardon, and enrol in the toughest revolutionary force there is, under the finest leader ever? Or are you content to contract out of adventure, and remain like so many other conformists, on the side of the Establishment, of social and financial conservatism, but without Christ the radical?

CHAPTER FIVE

RUNNING AWAY FROM CHRIST

IN A RECENT opinion poll, 94 per cent of the people of Great Britain claimed that they believed in a personal God. But how many of them do anything about him? Almost everybody prays to God in moments of danger, bereavement or crisis. But how many bother about him at other times? Very few. There is a widespread retreat from religion going on in the Western world at the present time. Undoubtedly the church is partly to blame for this; it has been defensive, inward-looking, lacking in social concern, cowardly in speaking out about moral issues, and sometimes reluctant to face the truth. The church has gone a long way to make Christianity incredible. It is the church, not Jesus Christ, that is the main stumbling-block for ordinary people.

But when all this is said, and it must be said with deep humility by any honest Christian, the current drift from Christianity is culpable. A great many people who are all too ready to dismiss religion with a wave of the hand are themselves unwilling to face up to the challenge of Jesus Christ. If Christianity is wrong about our origin or destiny, the purpose and the meaning of life, the value of persons and the secret of living together in community, then get up and say so! Say it violently, aggressively if you like: but say it *after you have personally examined the evidence.* Yet this is precisely what so many are apparently too afraid or too lazy to do. On matters of such vital importance they are content to be guided by scraps of information gleaned long ago in the Sunday school, by the latest newspaper attack on the faith, or by the voice and visiting habits of the local clergy!

I am convinced that the modern apathy about Christianity is nothing less than escapism. People are afraid of facing up to the challenge of Christian standards of behaviour and Christian discipleship. Have you noticed how people avoid sitting next to the man with the dog-collar in a bus or train? How some of the most militant atheists in a university simply dare not go along to a Christian meeting? How many a working man is literally terrified of being seen entering a church? Behind all these attitudes lies fear; fear of having to be reminded about the God we would much rather forget; fear of having to let our lives be scrutinized and spring-cleaned by God; fear of what other people would say if we came out on the side of Jesus Christ. It is much easier, much more comfortable, to run away.

Escape routes

There are many forms of this escapism current in today's world. It by no means springs always from a conscious attempt to run away from God; often it is the mess the world is in, the mess society is in, the mess our individual lives are in which drives us to take refuge in a fantasy world.

Sex is an obvious way of escape. You have only to go down a London Underground escalator to see advertisement after advertisement which shouts at you 'Sex satisfies. Sex is the way to fulfilment'. But it isn't as simple as that. Not for centuries has there been such overt emphasis on sex as the panacea for all human ills; but what have we to show for it? A sharp rise in VD, in illegitimate births, in psychological disturbances. Nor is this half the story. While Dr Leach is running down the value of the family, and Dr James Henning and his like advocate promiscuity, three-quarters of a million young people in England at any one time are the children of broken homes; and from their number something like 80 per cent of criminal offences come. The result is that we have the highest crime rate in our history; among the under twenties it has doubled in nine years; the prisons are so overcrowded that three people have to share a single cell, and Quarter Sessions have to sit on an average not four times a year, as in the past, but ten. These are the realities of the situation to which a judge drew my attention recently. They are deliberately ignored by many young people (and not so young, too) who selfishly and irresponsibly seek a gateway into Wonderland through extra-marital sex.

The same two charges of irresponsibility and selfishness apply to another notorious form of escapism, the ever increasing drug habit. Talk to people who are hooked on heroin. They will tell you that they don't care about anyone else—all they care about is where their next fix is coming from. And why shouldn't they? It's their life. If they want to wreck it in this way, why should anyone try to stop them? This is how they argue. It is sheer escapism, running away from the harsh realities of life into the cosy world of make-believe and the pleasant sensations induced by the drug.

Malcolm Muggeridge gave a scathing exposure of these two forms of escapism when he resigned from the Rectorship of Edinburgh University in protest against the clamour for contraceptive pills to be made available to all students. This he called 'the old slob's escapes of dope and bed'. He went on, 'the permissive morality of our time will, I am sure, reach its apogee. When birth pills are handed out with the free orange juice, and consenting adults wear special ties and blazers, and abortion and divorce. . . . are freely available on the public health, then at last, with the suicide rate up to Scandinavian proportions and the psychiatric wards bursting at the seams, it will be realized that this path is a disastrous cul-de-sac.' And he solemnly asserted that 'whatever life is or is not about, it is not to be expressed in terms of drugged stupefaction or casual sexual relations'.

Another form of escapism, to which the Beatles gave a boost when for a time they got involved in it, is Eastern meditation. This stands in striking contrast to Christian mysticism which encourages meditation upon and communion with the personal God of the Bible, not in order to escape from the responsibilities of daily life, but in order to face them with love and compassion for others. Christianity has no use for any supposed communion with God which does not transform the character of the worshipper and drive him out with God's own love and concern for men. The holy men of India have for centuries been practising a type of meditation which withdraws them from the concerns of daily life, and makes them parasites on the community, supported in their idleness by the gifts of the faithful. A Welsh correspondent writing to a national newspaper on the subject put this point very forcibly: 'No wonder that those who meditate feel peaceful, simple and calm. Disregard the world about you and you have nothing to worry about. It is this self-abstraction which is the product of meditation that has landed India in its present state of semi-starvation. Five thousand years of meditation have never ploughed a field or built a house.'

Many people run away from the challenge of authentic Christianity by a very different path. They become conformists; conformists to the shreds of post-Christian decencies and good deeds that still linger around the contemporary ethical scene. They may go to church occasionally — even to Communion, particularly at Christmas and Easter, without having the least belief in what it is all about. Ask them why they go, and they say, 'It makes me feel good.' This is not, I think, hypocrisy. It is simply a form of laziness — the reluctance to face up to the person of Jesus Christ, and decide, like a man, for him or against him. Others try to escape the condemnation of their own conscience by acts of great generosity, or by going to work in the slums for a while. Admirable in a way—but escapism all the same. Running away from God by trying to be decent is a very old expedient. Saul of Tarsus had been doing it for years before his own conversion. So had the poet Francis Thompson. He spoke for many escapists when he wrote:

> *I fled Him down the nights and down the days;*
> *I fled Him down the arches of the years;*
> *I fled Him down the labyrinthine ways*
> *Of my own mind, and in the mist of tears*
> *I hid from Him, and under running laughter.*

And all the time he heard a Voice, 'All things betray thee, who betrayest Me', 'Naught shelters thee who wilt not shelter Me', 'Naught contents thee who content'st not Me'. It was only when he had given in to the 'Hound of Heaven' that he discovered the mistake he had been making all the time. 'Thou dravest Love from thee, who dravest Me.'

There is no shortage of escape routes from reality; for reality seems to be a stimulant which we are able to take only in small doses. We are adept at devising ways of avoiding having to face up too often to fundamental issues. Gambling, drink and smoking are three such methods, with plenty of adherents; together they account in Britain for some £2,500 million a year—the equivalent of the defence budget before devaluation and withdrawal from East of Suez! The devising of scientific Utopias is another popular diversion for running away from reality. The 'Men Like Gods' school tells us with boundless enthusiasm of the joys of the technological future when, delivered from the old restraints of religion and conventional morality, and controlled by eugenics and euthanasia and all the other edifying things determined for us by the Guardians, human nature will reach an unprecedented stature. Fantasies like this looked jaded by the end of H. G. Wells's life; today, with the world hovering on the brink of extinction, they are puerile.

The most popular escape route from reality is the rat race. Get out from school into a well-paid job. Get more money, better prospects. Get a car, and a house and a wife. Get a family and a better house and a second car. Get promotion. Get a good pension . . . and then fill your life up with as much as you can before you die. Whatever you do, don't allow yourself time to wonder what life is all about. It might be too depressing a thought. That is the way a great many people behave, though when you set it down in cold print it looks peculiarly foolish. To turn one's back on human origin and destiny, human purpose and value, is surely escapism that verges on the frivolous. Yet those who adopt this irresponsible attitude to life are frequently heard to complain that the Christians are the runaways!

The inescapable Christ

There is nothing new about this accusation. It was the same in the first century. Peter writes to his scattered congregations in these terms: 'Indeed your former companions may think it very queer that you will no longer join with them in their riotous excesses, and accordingly say all sorts of unpleasant things about you. Don't worry: they are the ones who will have to explain their behaviour before the one who is prepared to judge all men, whether living or dead' (1 Peter 4:4, 5, Phillips). Peter's point is very apposite. Whatever the escape route from reality men choose, it will not do. The God of truth, the God who is real, will not allow them to live a lie for ever. In the end illusions will be stripped away, and truth will catch up with us all. The psalmist knew he could never escape from God's presence, hide where he would (Psalm 139).

The prophet knew that one day God would confront those who have made lies their refuge. Their shelter would be engulfed as the hail of truth beat in upon them (Isaiah 28:14–17). This awesome exposure to reality will hurt the church as much as anyone else. It will stand convicted of its lack of care for those who are not Christians, of its shameful introversion, of its pathetic tinkering with canons and liturgy while society decayed around it. Every refuge of lies will be stripped away, and every falsehood unmasked. Those who have made the church their escape route from reality will be exposed to the truth of Jesus Christ. As Peter put it, 'For the time has come for judgment to begin with the household of God' (1 Peter 4:17).

But that statement of Peter's continues: 'and if it (judgment) begins with us, what will be the end of those who do not obey the gospel of God?' They, too, will be brought face to face with the inescapable Christ. They too will be assessed by the Ideal Man from whom they have been running away. And what convincing excuses will they have to offer? 'I didn't believe you ever existed'? What utter nonsense; what culpable ignorance of the evidence! 'I didn't think your life was attractive enough, noble enough'? What manifest hypocrisy: it was rather that the standards of the man of Nazareth were too high, too costly, was it not? Or shall the excuse be simply 'I did not bother'? How do you think that will look to the Son of God, who became man for you, lived and died for you, rose again in order to take over your life and make a new man of you? No, all excuses will wither and wilt before the truth, the love, the self-sacrifice of Jesus. Final truth about the world, mankind and God has been disclosed by the Other who came into our very midst, the one who declared 'I am the truth'. By our relations to him we shall be judged, every one of us. There will come a final day of reckoning when it will be plain what answer we have returned to the question with which Pontius Pilate toyed, and tried unsuccessfully to evade: 'What will you do with Jesus?'

Time for action

If you mean to come to terms honestly with that question, may I make two suggestions? If you are not convinced that Jesus is the Truth, then read a Gospel. Read it slowly, thoughtfully, imaginatively. Ask yourself how you would expect Jesus to speak and act if he was mad, or a deceiver, or, alternatively, if he was what he claimed to be. Read it, think about it, and pray to God to show you if it is true or not. Above all, be prepared to follow Jesus if you are convinced about him. God will not give his light for you to trifle with. Jesus once explained the point in these words, to people who were incredulous about his claims and sceptical about his person: 'If any man's will is to do his (God's) will, he shall know whether the teaching is from God or whether I am speaking on my own authority' (John 7:17).

But many of you who read these words have already got beyond this stage. You need no further convincing about Jesus. You believe about him — but you don't know him. And you never will, until you yield your *will* to him, and ask him to take you and make what he wants of you. Without that decision on your part he will not dream of invading the privacy of your personality. God respects your will even when you exercise it against him. He waits for you to act. He has acted: he made you, he sustains you daily, he died for you, he is willing to come into your very being and share the future with you. He will . . . *if you will*. Pray to him, perhaps something like this: 'O Lord, I have been running away from you for a long time. I have tried to escape your challenge by going my own way. I admit I am to blame. I am prepared for a new start, from now on sharing my life with you, you who gave your life for me. Please come into my heart and life, as you promised you would.' To say that honestly, and to mean it, is to pass through the gateway into adventurous and immensely rewarding Christian living. Dare you do it? Or are you going to take the coward's way out, and continue running away from Christ?

FOR FURTHER READING

I RUNNING AWAY FROM HISTORY

J. N. D. Anderson, *Christianity: the witness of history* (Tyndale Press, 1969).

F. F. Bruce, *The New Testament Documents*. 5th ed. (Inter-Varsity Press, 1960).

C. H. Dodd, *The Apostolic Preaching and its Developments* (Hodder and Stoughton, 1944).

C. H. Dodd, *The Founder of Christianity* (Collins, 1971).

C. H. Dodd, *History and the Gospel* (Hodder Christian Paperbacks, 1964).

A. M. Hunter, *Paul and his Predecessors*. 2nd ed. (SCM Press, 1961).

F. G. Kenyon, *The Bible and Archaeology* (Harrap, 1940).

J. Klausner, *Jesus of Nazareth* (Allen and Unwin, 1925).

W. M. Ramsay, *The Bearing of Recent Discovery on the Trustworthiness of the New Testament* (Hodder and Stoughton, 1915).

W. M. Ramsay, *St. Paul the Traveller and Roman Citizen* (Hodder and Stoughton, 1920).

H. H. Rowley, *The Dead Sea Scrolls and the New Testament* (SPCK, 1957).

A. Rendle Short, *Archaeology Gives Evidence*. Revised ed. by A. R. Millard (Inter-Varsity Press, 1962).

M. A. Smith, *From Christ to Constantine* (Inter-Varsity Press, 1971).

J. A. Thompson, *The Bible and Archaeology* (Paternoster Press, 1963).

H. E. W. Turner, *Historicity and the Gospels* (Mowbrays, 1963).

2 RUNNING AWAY FROM SCIENCE

R. L. F. Boyd, *Can God be Known?* (Inter-Varsity Press, 1967).

C. A. Coulson, *Science and Christian Belief* (Fontana, 1958).

J. N. Hawthorne, *Questions of Science and Faith.* Revised ed. (Inter-Varsity Press, 1972).

M. A. Jeeves, *The Scientific Enterprise and Christian Faith* (Tyndale Press, 1969).

C. E. M. Joad, *Recovery of Belief* (Faber, 1952).

D. M. MacKay, *Christianity in a Mechanistic Universe* (Inter-Varsity Press, 1965).

D. M. MacKay, *Science and Christian Faith Today* (Falcon, 1960).

J. B. Phillips, *Ring of Truth* (Hodder Christian Paperbacks, 1967).

J. B. Torrance and others, *Where Science and Faith Meet* (Inter-Varsity Press, 1953).

3 RUNNING AWAY FROM REALITY

Communism, humanism

J. C. Bennett, *Christianity and Communism Today.* Revised ed. (SCM Press, 1961).

M. Bourdeaux, *Faith on Trial in Russia* (Hodder Christian Paperbacks, 1971).

M. Bourdeaux, *Opium of the People* (Faber, 1965).

Douglas Hyde, *I Believed* (World's Work, 1961).

T. M. Kitwood, *What is Human?* (Inter-Varsity Press, 1970).

Eugène Lyons, *Workers' Paradise Lost* (Longmans, 1967).

D. M. MacKay, *Humanism, Positive and Negative* (Inter-Varsity Press, 1966).

Nikita Struve, *Christians in Contemporary Russia* (Harvill, 1967).

FOR FURTHER READING

Psychology

D. Stafford Clark, *Psychiatry Today* (Penguin, 1953).

M. A. Jeeves, *Scientific Psychology and Christian Belief* (Inter-Varsity Press, 1967).

D. M. Lloyd-Jones, *Conversions: Psychological and Spiritual* (Inter-Varsity Press, 1959).

H. L. Philp, *Freud and Religious Belief* (Rockliff, 1956).

H. C. Rümke, *The Psychology of Unbelief* (Rockliff, 1952).

F. A. Schaeffer, *Escape from Reason* (Inter-Varsity Press, 1968).

W. B. Selbie, *Christianity and the New Psychology* (Bles, 1939).

4 RUNNING AWAY FROM ADVENTURE

J. N. D. Anderson, *The Evidence for the Resurrection* (Inter-Varsity Press, 1950).

Robert Crossley, *We Want to Live* (Inter-Varsity Press, 1967).

Michael Green, *Man Alive!* (Inter-Varsity Press, 1967).

H. Loukes, *Teenage Religion* (SCM Press, 1961).

F. Morison, *Who Moved the Stone?* (Faber, 1930).

A. M. Ramsey, *The Resurrection of Christ* (Bles, 1945).

David Watson, *My God is Real* (Falcon, 1970).

5 RUNNING AWAY FROM CHRIST

Michael Green, *Choose Freedom* (Inter-Varsity Press, 1965).

John Stott, *Basic Christianity.* Revised ed. (Inter-Varsity Press, 1971).

D. Swann, *A Faith that is Real* (Inter-Varsity Press, 1968).

J. Young, *The Case against Christ* (Falcon, 1971).